Publish and Prosper:
Blogging for Your Business

DL Byron and Steve Broback

New
Riders

Publish and Prosper: Blogging for Your Business

DL Byron and Steve Broback

New Riders
1249 Eighth Street
Berkeley, CA 94710
510/524-2178
800/293-9444
510/524-2221 (fax)

Find us on the Web at www.newriders.com
To report errors, please send a note to errata@peachpit.com

New Riders is an imprint of Peachpit, a division of Pearson Education

Acquisitions Editor: Michael Nolan
Project Editors: Kristin Mellone Kalning, Ted Waitt
Development Editor: Davina Baum
Production Editor: Tracey Croom
Copyeditor: Joanne Gosnell
Compositor: Diana Van Winkle, Van Winkle Design
Indexer: Jack Lewis
Cover Design: Aren Howell
Interior Design: Diana Van Winkle, Van Winkle Design

Notice of Rights

Notice of Liability

Trademarks

ISBN 0-321-39538-7
987654321
Printed and bound in the United States of America

Acknowledgments

DL Byron:

The book was authored with much help from Teresa Valdez Klein, Davina Baum, Kristin Kalning, Michael Nolan, Kim Larsen, Erin Kissane, and the rest of the staff at Peachpit.

Due props to Scott Benish and Wesley Pierce for their work on Clip-n-Seal and to all the fact-checking, idea discussions, and general instant messaging conversations with Timothy Appnel, Eric Rice, Cameron Barrett, Drew McLellan, Mike Davidson, Anil Dash, Lenn Pryor, Jason Fried, Jim Coudal, Doug Manis, Shaun Inman, Toby Malina, Matthew Oliphant, Frank Steele, Jason Swihart, Mie Yaginuma, Jeremy Wagstaff, D. Keith Robinson, Nick Finck, and Shel Israel.

Special thanks to Jeffrey Zeldman for starting me on the book path and to the rest of the Blog Business Summit co-founders Brian Alvey, Glenn Fleishman, Molly E. Holzschlag, Robert Scoble, and Dave Taylor. Also thanks to Chris Brownrigg, Dave Weitz, Jim Condoles, Shannon Fowler, and Fritz Johnston at Boeing.

Of course, the book wouldn't have happened without my co-author Steve Broback and the blogosphere.

For all those hours I spent in the Richland Public Library as a kid, reading books randomly from the shelves and studying obscure words in the Oxford English Dictionary, I'm grateful.

Steve Broback:

Special thanks to Robert Scoble, Glenn Fleishman, and Molly E. Holzschlag for bringing me into the wonderful world of blogging. My writings would never have been conceived without their gracious tutoring.

The Blog Business Summit team: Kim Larsen, DL Byron, Maryam Scoble, Krista Carreiro, Jason Preston, Eric Anderson, David Lake, and Teresa Valdez Klein.

Summit speakers and blogging gurus who have taught me so much: Jeffrey Zeldman, Buzz Bruggeman, Debbie Weil, Halley Suitt, Dave Taylor, Biz Stone, Mary Hodder, Matt Mullenweg, Lenn Pryor, Janet Johnson, Eric Rice, Dori Smith, Jeff Angus, Anil Dash, and Mie Yaginuma.

Supporters of our blogs and events: Shannon Fowler, Fritz Johnston, Jason Swihart, Tom Peters, Margaret Cobb, Dean Hachamovitch, Alan Nusbaum, and dozens of other people and organizations that have helped us along the way.

Long time co-conspirators and family: My parents, Julie and Kip Myers, Jim Heid, Toby Malina, Steve Roth, Jon Fitch, and Larry Westfall.

The production and editorial team at Peachpit: Marjorie Baer, Michael Nolan, Kristin Kalning, Erin Kissane, Rebecca Ross, Davina Baum, Tracey Croom, Ted Waitt, Diana Van Winkle, and Joanne Gosnell.

Thanks to my co-author DL Byron whose insights and knowledge made this book an effort I am proud to be associated with.

Last and far from least, special production and editorial kudos to Teresa Valdez Klein, who worked so hard and contributed so much toward making this book (and our many blog sites) a reality.

Table of Contents

Chapter 5   **Tools and Implementation** **83**

Chapter 1

Meet the Blogs

It seems as though everywhere you turn, people are talking about blogs: news blogs, blogs about travel, sports blogs, celebrity blogs. The term *weblog* (later shortened to *blog*) was coined in 1997, but it didn't come into popular use until 2000. By 2004, it was the *Merriam-Webster Dictionary*'s word of the year, and blogs now receive coverage in every major newspaper and business magazine in the United States.

Businesses have recently begun to understand the potential benefits of blogging. By providing companies with an unprecedented opportunity to engage with customers in a conversation, blogs can help companies research new products, sell their wares, extend their brands, and engage with customers.

What Exactly Is a Blog?

How are blogs different from any other Web site? And why are major corporations and small businesses all over the world falling all over themselves to start blogging? Most importantly, how will they help *your* business?

Fear not. This chapter will not only explain what makes a blog a blog, but also why they benefit the businesses that employ them. We're going to show you how blogs can allow your business to engage individual readers, connect with strong social networks, and get the attention of the world's most powerful search tools, all in one go.

Most blogs share a set of features that set them apart from other kinds of Web sites. As you'll see in **Figure 1.1**, a blog typically includes:

- Content entries or "posts," presented in chronological order (newest content on top), with each post also archived at a permanent URL. Permanent archives of individual posts encourage other bloggers to link to your posts. The author of the post, date, and category are also presented. We'll discuss post content and style in Chapter 6, "Writing Your Blog."

- A reader comments section that allows bloggers and readers to converse. A comments section requires a resource commitment, but can also promote a lively conversation with your readers. You'll find a detailed discussion of the risks and benefits of reader comments in Chapter 4, "Designing for Readers," and advice on comment monitoring in Chapter 8, "Monitoring and Managing Your Blog."

- A subscription feature called "RSS" or "syndication" that allows readers to subscribe to a blog and be alerted automatically when the site updates. Syndication can substantially increase your readership, and we'll discuss it in detail in Chapter 4.

- Topical archives for organizing posted content. For large blogs with thousands of posts, archives can also be organized by month, year, and keyword. Searches are also offered to help readers find what they're looking for. All of these archives are generated automatically by your blogging software, and we'll also discuss archiving strategies in Chapter 4.

There are other subtler distinctions between blogs and conventional Web sites. We'll discuss the types of content and the informal writing style typically associated with blogging in Chapter 6.

While all of these features *can* be built into a non-blog Web site, a blog engine is purpose-built. The benefit of using specialized blogging software is that it's inexpensive and designed specifically to make it easy for non-programmers and non-designers to take advantage of these features.

Figure 1.1

The anatomy of a blog, using *www.inflighthq.com* as an example. The diagram shows essential features of a blog and a 2-column layout.

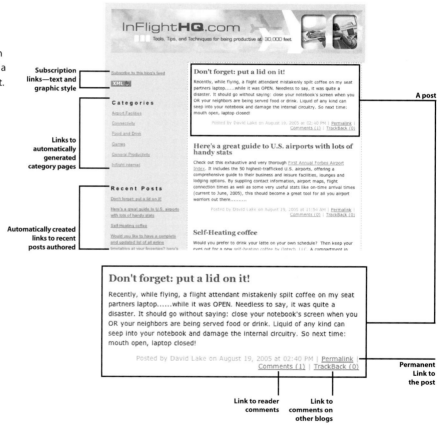

How Did We Get Here?

You may remember some of the very early Web pages, with gray backgrounds, black text, and blue links. Then came along images, sound, animated graphics, and bits of video, but they were still essentially static. Even when some sites began using databases to create "dynamic sites" that separated the content from the code, the content still only changed when someone got around to updating it.

There were also administrative and workflow problems: What if you wanted to allow staff members to edit some pages, but not others? What if you needed non-technical people to add content to your site? For large sites with daily update schedules like the *New York Times* Web site, hand-production of each page was simply impossible.

Many large organizations solved those problems by purchasing content management systems (CMSs) that made it easier for non-technical staff members to enter and edit content that lived in a database. After training their employees, companies could allow staff members to create new pages based on templates and to make changes to multiple pages by altering a single file. The downside was that many of these systems were too expensive and difficult to learn to make them useful for individuals and smaller businesses.

Enter the Blog

Beginning in the late 1990s, blogging software and services emerged that made it easy for anyone with a Web connection to create a Web site and update it frequently. Instead of laying out a page in HTML and manually positioning your content on it, all you had to do was enter your new content into a form and let the blogging software place the entry at the top of an automatically generated page. Quick, easy, and very inexpensive.

Incidentally, many of these blog services have become so sophisticated that they can now function as excellent and inexpensive CMSs; in fact, some free blog systems contain critical features that are missing from systems costing thousands of dollars.

Types of Blogs

But aren't blogs just a way for people to talk about their cats and family vacations? Not anymore.

Early bloggers created personal blogs that mirrored their own interests and Web-browsing habits. These blogs covered topics ranging from tech news to knitting—often on the same blog. Many functioned as online journals and dealt with highly personal topics, while others dealt with subjects of professional interest to their author (or authors, in the case of group blogs), as shown in **Figures 1.2a and 1.2b**.

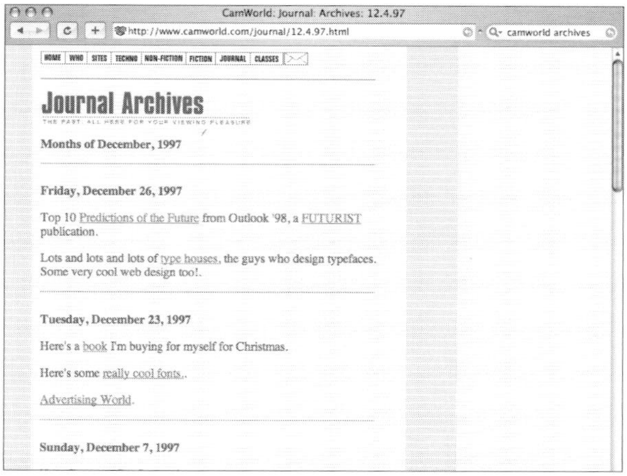

Figure 1.2a

CamWorld (*www. camworld.com*), a pioneering early blog, included a mix of Web design news, personal reflections, and cool links.

Figure 1.2b

Rebecca's Pocket (*www.rebeccablood.net*), another example of a personal blog.

Many businesses and other organizations have recently discovered that blogging can help them reach their internal and external communication goals. Even though they may use the same software as individual bloggers, businesses have a whole new set of objectives and concerns. Furthermore, business blogs can vary dramatically in purpose, focus, and feature offerings. Here are the general categories of blogs we've seen and worked with.

Company Blogs

A company blog, like those shown in **Figures 1.3a and 1.3b**, is about your business in general; it works like a brochure site, but with a blog for news, announcements, and other fresh content. It's typically limited to content about the company itself.

Figure 1.3a

The Boeing blog (*www. boeing.com/randy/*) is a good example of a general company blog.

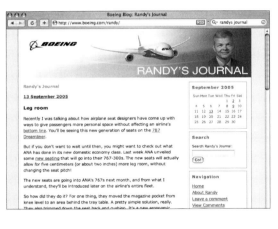

Figure 1.3b

A blog for the LiftPort Group (*www.liftport.com*), a smaller company that's building a space elevator.

Product Blogs

A product blog specifically promotes an item or service. Product blogs may overlap with brand blogs, but their primary purpose is to promote and sell. **Figures 1.4a and 1.4b** show good examples of product blogs.

Figure 1.4a

Clip-n-Seal (*www.clip-n-seal.com*) promotes its product, a bag-closure device, via its blog.

Figure 1.4b

Clothing retailer Bluefly uses its blog, Flypaper (*www.flypaper.bluefly.com*), for e-commerce.

Brand Blogs

A brand blog, as shown in **Figures 1.5a and 1.5b**, is used to communicate marketing messages and extend a company's brand into new markets and audiences. Boeing, GM Fastlane, Microsoft, and Sun all publish brand blogs. Some brand blogs are set up as sponsored blogs written by people outside the company.

Figure 1.5a

Microsoft has successfully communicated public relations messages through a blog written by Robert Scoble (*www. scoble.weblogs.com*), a Microsoft employee. Note how prominent the blog-specific search is on the Microsoft Community Blogs (*www.microsoft.com*).

Figure 1.5b

Connexion by Boeing, blogs without blogging by sponsoring inFlightHQ (*www. inflighthq.com*).

Blogs as a Business

Some blogs (shown in **Figures 1.6a, 1.6b, and 1.6c**) have transformed themselves into businesses. The Coudal (*www.coudal.com*) and SimpleBits (*www.simplebits.com*) blogs are good examples of blogs that initially focused on content and now sell ad space or products. Dilbert's creator Scott Adams started his own blog to promote the comic and sell subscriptions. As blogging matures and business models emerge, you'll find more bloggers quitting their day jobs to blog full-time.

Figure 1.6a

Coudal.com is a Web site and blog for Coudal Partners, a design and advertising firm. The site has evolved into a launchpad for several additional business ventures by building from the reader community that formed around the site and blog. From a design perspective, the Coudal.com blog is fully integrated into the larger site.

Figure 1.6b

SimpleBits is a Web design studio founded by Web designer and author Dan Cederholm. The SimpleBits blog is a combination personal/ professional blog that now promotes books and other products.

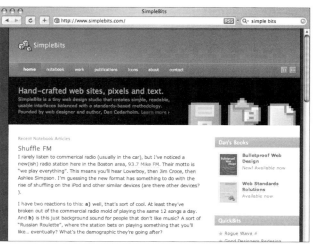

Figure 1.6c

Web design magazine A List Apart (*www. alistapart.com*) started as a mailing list and now has advertisers and a store. They also host conferences. (ALA offers many bloggy features such as syndication, frequent postings, and comments, but doesn't fit the literal definition of a blog. As discussed in Chapter 4, you can integrate blog features into your existing site.)

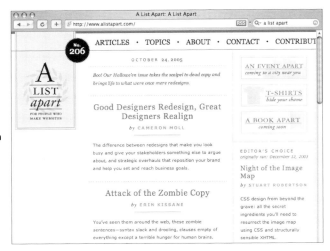

As you can see, many business blogs cross over into multiple categories—and change over time as business and audience needs evolve. By now you should have a good idea of what blogs are, how they came to be, and how businesses use them. But one major question remains: why it matters to *you*.

Businesspeople frequently ask us, "Why should my business blog?" With good planning and clear strategy, the benefits of blogging clearly outweigh the risks, so the real question becomes, "Why not?"

Why Should You Blog?

A quick analogy may be useful. Say that you own a storefront coffee shop on a side street that gets modest traffic. Your landlord offers you a larger store in a corner spot on Main Street for less money—and he'll throw in a new top-of-the-line espresso machine for free. You'd be crazy not to take the offer.

For most businesses, the choice to embrace blogging is a lot like this coffee shop scenario: more visibility, traffic, and the equivalent of an expensive CMS, all for very little money.

For almost zero financial investment in hardware or software, you can create a blog site that broadcasts your content to a potential audience of millions of people who use newsreader software. In addition, the naturally

"Google-friendly" architecture of blogs guarantees that search engines will pay more attention to what you publish.

An additional benefit is that your customers and potential customers can contribute additional valuable content to your site via their comments. They provide an entrée into a global ecosystem of bloggers and cross-linked blog conversations, which allows you to build buzz and reach out to hundreds of thousands of readers.

GreenCine is a company that rents DVDs online and relies heavily on their blog to drive sales. The GreenCine Daily blog (*www.daily.greencine.com*) draws over 2500 visitors a day who are interested in their coverage of independent and alternative cinema. Although owner Dennis Woo was originally skeptical that blogging would noticeably enhance their bottom line, he now says blogging is "core to our strategy" and credits the blog with helping double his company's sales in 2004.

Landfair Furniture is a small business run by Mike and Bev Landfair in Portland, Oregon. Mike and Bev decided to try blogging in hopes that it would drive traffic to their online site and boost awareness of their store. In just a few months of posting, they reported that the blog (*www.landfairfurniture.blogspot.com*) had definitely enhanced sales. As Mike Landfair says, "In an economy that still seems a little slow, our traffic to our main store has increased, and sales are up a healthy percentage over last year."

During the first three months of posting to her blog (*www.nhydefineart. typepad.com*), Colorado artist Nicole Hyde claims sales through the site were three times that of her physical gallery. When asked to compare the real and virtual outlets, Hyde says, "So far the blog's winning."

Let's take a more in-depth look at these benefits so you can get a better idea of the ways blogging can benefit *your* business.

Blogging Is Easy

When we speak about business blogging, we see a lot of eyes glaze over when we talk about the benefits—until we demonstrate, live and on stage, how easy it actually is to use a blog to publish content. Blogs are a revolutionary force because they're so incredibly easy to use.

In fact, publishing Web content has never been easier. In a recent BBC interview, Internet pioneer Sir Tim Berners-Lee described how blogging is closer to his original idea for the Web than what we use today: "What happened with blogs and with wikis, these editable Web spaces, was that they became much more simple. When you write a blog, you don't write complicated hypertext, you just write text, so I'm very, very happy to see that now it's gone in the direction of becoming more of a creative medium." (We'll discuss wikis, a close relation to blogs, in Chapter 9, "Beyond Blogging.")

As Berners-Lee says, blogs facilitate creativity. For businesses, that means you can concentrate on your messages, product launches, ideas, and conversations with your market. You're not using resources to write HTML or code a CMS; instead, you're using them to talk about your business and communicate with your customers.

Add and Update Content in a Snap

The ah-ha! moment for most new bloggers happens when they realize how fast and automated blogging is. Fill out a Web form, press Save, and your blog is updated. And without extra work, your blog has also updated your archives to include your new content, created a new comments section, and (if you're using syndication) informed your readers that there's new content waiting for them.

Because updating is so easy, you can concentrate on your content—and you should. Fresh content is the number-one thing that differentiates blogs from other Web sites. Unlike Web sites that are updated once a quarter at best, blogs offer new content quite frequently. Many update daily or several times a day, while others add new content once or twice a week.

Fresh content keeps readers (and search engines) coming back to your site regularly instead of visiting only when they need a specific piece of information. Content is the core of any successful business blog, and the other blog features we'll discuss are designed to maximize your reader's engagement with your content.

Get High-Power Features on a Low-Level Budget

The phrase "content management system" conjures up images of laptop-toting IT consultants, hundreds of thousands of dollars in expenses, and a system that is never used because employees hate it. Blogs haven't replaced big CMSs, but they do provide a lot of the functionality of a CMS in a flexible and inexpensive way.

One of the great things about posting or contributing to a blog is that it really requires little to no instruction or training. This is in contrast to a high-end CMS, where training is typically a requirement for all involved. People who blog know that posting a new article is as easy as writing and sending an email, and some blog systems let you post using your favorite email program. If you know how to write a subject line and a message, and can press a Send button, you can post a blog. We often tell people that blogging is like "sending an email to the world."

The better blog systems can be extended via software plug-ins or modules so that they can take on more advanced CMS features if need be. That way, things like permission-based publishing and workflow can be added later— it's the Lego™ building blocks approach to CMS design. You probably won't run a giant e-commerce site or a magazine with a blog, but it can allow you to add new sites and site extensions quickly and easily.

Broadcast Your Content Automatically

Blogs can broadcast their content via "RSS feeds." RSS stands for Real Simple Syndication, and *simple* is the key word. This technology, which is built into most blogging systems and applications, allows people to subscribe to your blog the way they'd subscribe to a newsletter—without you doing any extra work or managing a list of subscribers.

The easiest way to understand syndication is to think of the email newsletters that some companies publish. The business builds and manages an ever-changing subscriber list, writes special newsletter content, sends the content via email, and hopes people read it.

One of the most interesting things people discover when they start a blog with syndication is how soon they get visitors. One person we know set up his blog and made an initial test post to see if the system worked. Ten minutes later, as he continued to work on the layout and colors of the page, he noticed that his traffic meter had already registered visitors coming to the site.

With blog syndication, you write your blog posts and customers who like them can subscribe to your blog (or to just specific topics they want to follow). These same customers will receive notification via their Web browser (in some cases) or special news-reading software when your blog is updated. Your messages don't get lost in email or mistaken for spam, your customers can read it when they want to, and it all drives traffic back to your site.

Syndication will continue to become more mainstream as more browsers support it natively. The Firefox browser also supports RSS, and the new version of Internet Explorer (7.0) will display RSS.

Blogs Are a Marketer's Dream

By analyzing public reaction to a blog, reading comments, and directly engaging the world of blogs and bloggers (informally known as the "blogosphere"), companies can gain access to a wealth of information about their market's opinion of them. By responding to comments, sponsoring or hosting blogs, and sometimes running their own company blogs, businesses can build, revive, and extend their brands.

There are many branding success stories in business blogging, even though the form is relatively new. Boeing's Connexion in-flight Internet service extended its marketing reach to the blogosphere by inviting bloggers to test its in-flight Internet service, and GM's Fastlane blog (*www.fastlane.gmblogs.com*) allows readers to converse directly with the company's vice chairman of global product development. Microsoft uses blogs to speak directly with their developers, rebuilding a relationship that has been strained in the past.

Later on, we'll talk more about these companies, and about new businesses that have built their brands mainly—or in one case, exclusively—using blogs. First, though, let's look at the reasons blogs work so well as a marketing and public-relations tool.

Readers *Like* Blogs

In the age of information overload, headlines and news blurbs that are short, focused, and written in conversational English are much appreciated by online readers. Additionally, it's now common for people to find answers to questions (and casual reading material) via search engines. Because blogs' simple structure, strong link networks, and fresh content appeal to search engines, it's often easier to find relevant blogged content than to find the same information on traditional Web pages. Many bloggers have found that their posts often rank higher in Google than the pages and sites they are writing about!

We discovered this ourselves when we posted about an editorial that *PC Magazine* had published on their site. Well-known columnist John Dvorak had written a piece about bloggers, and we wanted to respond by posting on our site. Later we discovered that if you type the words *Dvorak, utopianist,* and *bloggers* (three words that appeared in his article as well as our response), our post came up first in Google and his article came up seventh. In between were five other blogs. This was clearly a situation in which Google thought six blog posts commenting about an article were more relevant than the article itself. We're pretty sure that if the original article had not been posted on a traditional site and had been on a blog instead, it would have ranked higher.

Another easy test of this is to go into Google and type in the word *genuine.* As of this writing, Google says there are 58 million pages containing that word, including the highly ranked Genuine Microsoft Software page at Microsoft. com. What's at the top? A personal blog of course.

A final example comes from a competition held in 2004 in which hundreds of search engine consultants and experts competed to see who could make a page of their creation come to the top in Google when a predefined search term was entered. After two months of vigorous competition where aggressive tricks were employed (such as the creation of fake eBay auctions to help drive interest), the winner was declared. As you can guess, it was a blog entry. Unlike most other entries, blogger Anil Dash (*www.dashes.com*) had done nothing special to "optimize" his site. He just asked his readers to link back to him.

Most importantly, at least 20 million people worldwide (and this number is growing rapidly) get information delivered to them through RSS subscriptions. Blogs deliver info to these subscribers, and regular Web sites don't.

Here's a great example. *Car and Driver*'s Web site went live in 1997, years before Autoblog (*www.autoblog.com*), a competing Web site. Autoblog offers RSS, reader comments, and links to other sites that discuss its posts—tried-and-true blog features designed to generate lots of user traffic. All those bloggy features appear to be paying off: Alexa.com, a service that estimates Web traffic, currently shows Autoblog as outperforming its better-established rival.

A Genuine Conversation

Blogs are also engaging for readers because they provide a convenient forum for genuine dialogue. Successful blogs build on communication. Once your fresh content has attracted readers, you want to keep them engaged in the conversation you've started. Blogs provide a number of ways to encourage that.

JOIN A CONVERSATION

Conversations abound in the blogosphere on every imaginable topic. To find and join a conversation, try Technorati (*www.technorati.com*), a search engine for blogs and Intelliseek's Blogpulse (*www.blogpulse.com*), an automated trend discovery system for blogs. We'll talk more about how best to follow conversations in the blogosphere in Chapter 8.

Reader Comments

Most non-blog Web sites don't offer a way for people to comment on specific new content that you add to the site. Tenacious readers may hunt down your email address and send you their thoughts, but the conversation takes place in private, adding nothing to the vitality of your site. Discussion forums have been around for years, of course, but blogs have the advantage of a narrator who guides the flow of discussion and keeps the conversation flowing.

Blog comments add the voices of your readers to your posts and give you an opportunity to gain priceless insight about your market and its view of your products and your company. Incidentally, your readers' discussions also attract search engines, which in turn attract new readers.

Public discussions with your customers and other readers may seem risky, but the rewards are great. Later, we'll talk more about how to reduce risk and manage comments to create a thriving community.

Interaction with Other Bloggers

Blogging culture encourages conversations that start on one blog to spill over into others. Blog A discusses (and links to) a post on Blog B, and the readers of both blogs leave comments that link to other sites, spreading the conversation to ever more readers and creating the "buzz" that blogging is famous for.

There are a lot of little but important ways to encourage this kind of community interaction. Permanent URLs for each post let other bloggers link to your content, while the syndication/subscription system we mentioned above helps bloggers keep track of new content on your site so that they can comment on it and spread the word further.

In addition to individual features, though, you can foster interaction with other bloggers—and non-bloggers—by designing your blog with ease of use in mind, and most of all, by posting great content. We'll discuss both of those important factors in Chapters 4 and 6, respectively.

Search Engines Love Blogs

Search engines such as Google are biased in favor of sites that are updated on a regular basis, which makes blogs a natural when it comes to traffic generation.

Blogs' frequent updates and informal language produce an exceptionally search-friendly body of content, and many of the features that make blogs easier for humans to use (like permanent URLs and links to and from other blogs) also attract the attention of search engines and the people who use them. We'll go into the search-engine benefits of blogging in detail in Chapters 3 and 6—and we'll include tips on using blog structure and even writing style to make sure you're maximizing your blog's search-engine friendliness.

Why Shouldn't You Blog?

Many companies shy away from blogging because they associate the form with indiscretion and unbridled information sharing, and therefore fear that blogging employees will reveal trade secrets or embarrassing facts. It's a legitimate concern for some organizations, and public companies have to be especially vigilant not to reveal things that might put them in violation of SEC regulations.

That said, even these companies can choose a variant on the standard blogging approach and get the benefits of the blog architecture and ecosystem without risking a communications catastrophe.

A Blog Choice for Everyone

The range of corporate blogging approaches is quite extensive, and range widely in terms of manpower, as well as degree of risk to the company.

At the very least, your company should **monitor the blogosphere** for posts and comments that reference your organization. Equally important is for company representatives **to respond appropriately** to what's being said via email or comments. You're not actually blogging here, but you're contributing to the blogosphere. This approach also presents very little risk.

Another low-risk strategy is to **sponsor or host blogs** that contain editorial content that appeals to your potential and existing customers. This is what Boeing has done with the "inFlightHQ" blog we set up for them. inFlightHQ is not a blog specifically about Boeing or its products, but it does contain posts that business flyers find interesting. This approach also doesn't require the company to blog, and presents little risk.

One way to have a company actually blog yet not bear much risk or commitment is **to set up a blog that references key information** that has been put up on the organization's regular Web site. Items such as press releases and product announcements are a good fit for this type of blog. Odds are that over time this new mirror will ultimately get more traffic than your current site.

These approaches are almost completely risk free, but can produce huge dividends for any business that invests the minimal time and money required to implement them. They also can act as a training ground for the eventual move into a full-fledged customer dialog blog, which we suspect will be a mandatory transition for most companies in the long term.

The riskiest yet potentially the most powerful approach is to **host one or more blogs** that specifically discuss what the company or employees are doing. Many organizations have achieved huge visibility and PR gains from this commitment. This approach requires actual blogging, and needs careful thought and execution to minimize risk. This option is the most controversial and requires the most risk, attention, and effort.

YOU'RE PLAYING IN SOMEONE ELSE'S SANDBOX

The most experienced bloggers on the Web have been blogging for eight years—a lifetime, given the accelerated pace of the Internet. Blogs have been around long enough to develop their own system of etiquette, and if you barge in and ignore that system, you'll attract very public derision.

Happily, it's not a very complicated system, and bloggers tend to be forgiving of early mistakes. Bloggers and blog readers expect that if you start a blog, you'll treat it like a blog, not a press conference or a brochure site.

When Boeing launched Randy's Journal, many bloggers criticized them for running a "pseudo-blog" because the blog didn't offer the expected features, such as syndication and comments. Boeing addressed this criticism head-on and made a number of changes with our help. They also continued to make their own decisions about how to balance their business goals with the blogosphere's expectations. Their erstwhile critics gave Boeing credit for responding so openly, and Boeing learned how to handle themselves in the blogosphere.

In the next chapter, we'll help you define your plan for balancing business needs with the expectations of the blog work.

What's *Your* Blog Focus?

The dozens of companies we have talked to and worked with in the last few years have developed a myriad of strategies and tactics for using the blogosphere, but they've all had one thing in common: results. In every case, the return on investment of executing a smart blog strategy has been higher than that of nearly any other marketing initiative in the company.

The easiest way to learn about blogging is just to jump in and start paying attention to the blog world, and then to start participating. We always encourage the businesses we advise to start small—perhaps just paying attention to conversations between existing bloggers—and then scale up to whatever level of involvement makes sense to their organization.

One of the beautiful things about blogs is that they don't require a massive Web design project. They're small, nimble, and simply structured, so you can start your blog in a matter of hours and immediately begin playing with the medium. In the next chapters, we'll begin to look at the choices you need to make about your organization's approach to blogging and talk more about designing and developing a blog.

Chapter 2

Determining Your Focus

In Chapter 1, "Meet the Blogs," we made the case for how weblogs are proving effective in business. Now we'll take it one step further: How can your company enable the right blog(s), the right way?

As you know by now, blogs are ideal for reaching out to—and connecting with—your market. Thanks to syndication and commenting features, along with the preferential treatment given to blogs by search engines, most successful business blogs tend to be oriented toward customer outreach. Not surprisingly, the vast majority of the businesses that have approached us with blogging in mind hope to create sites that their target market will embrace. Since it's so easy to set up a blog and posts can cover almost any topic, it's a good idea to take some time and consider what you hope the blog will achieve. We'll be focusing here on strategies intended to create dialog with customers, potential customers, and market influencers.

Like the people who write them, no two blogs are exactly alike. Each one has its own personality, audience, and reason for being. To make your time and effort count, it's critical that you survey the possibilities and select the right direction for you and your team.

Business blogs can generally be broken down into three primary categories:

- Marketing–focused blogs are designed to build traffic, awareness, and sales.

- Public relations–focused blogs enhance image and influence public perception.

- Customer service–focused blogs assist and inform customers or potential customers.

While one blog can certainly contain posts covering any or all of these themes, it's a good idea to select one as the core focus for you and your team. Deciding on a central focus will help keep the content on-topic, and can make sure you are targeting the right audience. Since blogging should be interesting and fun for both bloggers and their readers, a clearly defined central theme that everyone understands will help ensure that there are few unpleasant surprises.

Let's look at these key categories and profile several examples for each. Hopefully you'll get some ideas for what might serve as the most appropriate model for your organization.

A Marketing Focus

Almost all businesses dedicate significant resources to understanding their market and spreading the word about their company and the products they offer. For many successful organizations, blogging has provided a crucial way to raise that awareness.

The Web is a critical channel for marketing and selling products and services. A 2005 survey of over 1000 leaders of small- and medium-sized businesses conducted by Interland indicated that 87 percent of those surveyed are receiving monthly revenue from their Web site. For many, blogs that focus on selling products are proving effective at generating revenue.

Taking care of current customers is good business. It's been well documented that one of the best resources a business has for driving future sales is their current customer base. According to Fredrick F. Reichheld, director of the strategy-consulting firm Bain & Company, a 5-percentage-point increase in customer retention in a typical company will increase profits by more than 25 percent. In addition, satisfied customers drive positive word of mouth buzz, which can strongly influence new customers. Blogs are proving to be a great way to support your customers after they've bought (and before they buy again).

These are four focus areas we suggest you consider for a marketing-related blog, and ones we'll discuss in more depth below.

- Blogs that help you understand and interact with your market

- Blogs that raise awareness and visibility

- Blogs that sell products

- Blogs that support current (and prospective) customers

Encouraging an Interactive Audience

We talk throughout this book about how blogs allow you to interact more directly with new, existing, and potential customers by giving them easy ways to talk with you, stay in touch, and be alerted whenever you post something new. This exchange allows you to increase awareness about your company and to sell products directly. Dialog also allows you to learn more about what your market wants—because customers will tell you, right in your blog.

Blogs and their inherent interactivity enable readers to "gather to discuss issues and ideas," claims reporter Brian Steinberg in a 2005 *Wall Street Journal* article. Bloggers are facilitating a "virtual focus group" where companies listen and respond to comments and then use that feedback to improve their products and support.

We've seen this ourselves—part of Clip-n-Seal's success has come from discovering new uses for our product from buyer comments. For example, customers told us how they used Clip-n-Seals for do-it-yourself vacuum forming and furniture veneering.

To get this type of focus group feedback, just enable comments on your blog, post about your product, and then ask for input. Newsvine, a Web startup that offers news written by a community of citizen journalists, did just that when they announced the unofficial early launch of their site. When they went beta with the service, they hosted a blog right along with it and asked readers to "kick the tires," and offer their feedback. This input resulted in several key modifications to the service prior to their official launch.

Mike Davidson, CEO of Newsvine (*blog.newsvine.com*), said, "The Newsvine blog was built to act as a virtual focus group, and the resulting input has been very valuable."

We'll learn more about Newsvine and their successful product launch in Chapter 7, "Launching Your Blog and Getting Noticed." We'll also teach you how to keep that buzz going.

The bottom line is that a blog that encourages lots of comments and reader participation will need frequent and ongoing monitoring. Authorizing comments, eliminating inappropriate contributions, and making sure the site's authors are participating in the discussion is crucial to keeping the dialog going. **Figure 2.1** shows the type of comments we get on the Blog Business Summit.

Figure 2.1

Many blog administration programs let you approve and moderate the comments that come in from readers.

TIP: Before you target dialog as a primary goal for your blog, make sure you have the staffing and time to do it right. For blogs like the Blog Business Summit, an hour or two of attention every day and frequent checking in on what's being said in the comments can go a long way to ensure that participation is managed correctly. Chapter 3, "How Much Blog—and How Often?," goes into resources in more detail.

Raising Awareness and Visibility

Smart marketers work hard to get their company and products talked about on the Web, with the ultimate goal of having their offerings found more often by people searching or surfing the Internet.

Blogs that get lots of visitors (traffic) have two key attributes that make them special. Those attributes are visibility and findability.

Visible sites are those that are mentioned frequently and, in many cases, are linked to and from many Web pages. Amazon is one of the most visible sites thanks to (among other things) their affiliate program, which pays people small commissions for routing paying customers their way. If you put a special Amazon link and graphic on your blog, you can make a little extra money, and Amazon gets another virtual "billboard" enhancing their visibility. Millions of blog pages have these little Amazon ads on them, and they drive significant traffic to Amazon.com.

It's clear that the more opportunities people have to click and visit, the more they will do so. Similarly with blogs, the more sites that mention your company or reference your posts, the more visible you will be.

Findable sites are those that search engines like Google feel are relevant and place at or near the top of search results pages. The evidence is overwhelming that the links near the top of a search results list get many more clicks than the ones at the bottom. These sites at the top have good "Google Juice," according to Web marketing geeks. Most bloggers who monitor their traffic statistics closely know that a significant number of the people coming to their site are clicking through from Google and other search results pages. It's pretty clear that the more relevant search engines think you are, the more visitors you'll get.

How does Google determine that one site is more relevant than another? In a nutshell, the answer is inbound links. If two sites have identical content, but one has more people linking to it, Google thinks it's a more "important" site. In general, a more linked-to site will come up higher in search results than one with fewer people linking to it.

 NOTE: If you're doing well on one search engine, you're doing well on the rest of them. Search engines use similar algorithms, and some use the same code or aggregate results, like dogpile.com, which is a meta search or a search of search engines. Clearly, the common goal for achieving visibility and findability is to get people to mention and link back to you. The path to success here is to write a lot (a whole lot) of interesting posts that bloggers pay attention to (and refer others to). The elaborate (and often expensive) linking strategies advocated by many Web marketing consultants is usually far less productive than just writing well about subjects that will grab your readers' attention.

LINKING FOR DOLLARS

Getting other sites and blogs to link back to you is vital if you want your blog to become a high-profile destination. Ever since marketers discovered that inbound links could help a site get traffic, services have cropped up that promise inbound links—for a price.

These "link brokers" claim that for as little as 50 cents a link, they can get you the inbound links you need to boost your traffic and search engine rankings. Using sites they've established along with compensated partners, these brokers can potentially create dozens or even hundreds of links back to your blog.

This visibility jump-start may sound inviting, but we tell clients to avoid these services and instead to focus their energies on writing about subjects that will get linked to naturally. Google is on the lookout for people trying to get links that they view as "illegitimate" and could conceivably determine your brokered links fit that profile. If Google senses your inbound links have been fabricated, they might actually move your site lower in rankings, or may even remove you from results pages completely. Do not try to be smarter than Google.

We'll cover specific writing techniques that will attract attention in Chapter 5, "Tools and Implementation," and Chapter 6, "Writing Your Blog," but as you plan your blog, be aware that you'll need to post frequently on subjects of interest to your target market and spend time encouraging those all-important inbound links.

Spreading the Word

Buzz Bruggeman is the founder and directs all marketing for the company that creates and sells ActiveWords, a computer-automation software application. Since 2003, Bruggeman has relied almost exclusively on his blog (*www.buzzmodo.typepad.com*) and fellow bloggers to spread the word about his product. His strategy has been to maximize his visibility on Google and other search engines through posts and relationships that generate inbound links. Bruggeman claims that his efforts to cultivate high-profile bloggers and the resulting inbound links have enhanced his findability significantly. He notes that one favorable post (and inbound link) from Robert Scoble delivered ten times the sales than a feature article in a national newspaper. Overall, Bruggeman's blogging strategy has boosted sales by more than 250 percent.

The bottom line is that blogs intended to raise awareness and visibility require frequent (and interesting) posts that are compelling enough that others will notice and link back to them. Run a travel agency? Think about posts with subjects like "How to Save 30 Percent on Every Flight You Book."

SEARCHERS ARE SHOPPERS

It's fairly well established that online commerce is big business. In 2005 alone, 82 billion dollars of goods and services were sold over the Internet.

What's less well-known is that important search engines, like Google, factor into consumer purchases. In 2005, a survey conducted by Harris Interactive revealed that most adult shoppers who research products online before making a purchase rely on search engines more than any other tool to assist them in their decision making.

Given the preferential treatment Google gives blogs in their search results—which we discussed in Chapter 1—it's fairly straightforward that an online retailer should be able to see a bottom-line benefit to posting about their offerings.

Closing Sales

Most of the bloggers we know who are experiencing success promoting products or services don't embrace the "hard sell" approach. Many of these people would chafe at the notion of actively trying to manipulate visitors, and would rather just focus on creating quality posts that get noticed. While we agree posts are great for driving traffic and credibility, sales will certainly be enhanced if you have a strategy for dealing with people once they arrive on your blog—and that doesn't mean breaking out the hard sell.

Experienced online retailers like Amazon and Land's End spend millions of dollars and thousands of hours annually trying to enhance "conversion rate," which is a measurement indicating what percentage of Web site visitors become buyers. Those companies have discovered scores of techniques (mostly proprietary) that can make a huge difference in sales. In a report issued in April 2005, Nielsen/NetRatings released an Internet retail analysis that indicated that for the top 100 Web retailers, an average of 1 in 20 visitors become buyers. Amazon's rate is more than double that. If you are averaging less than 5 percent conversion, you may want to look at ways to help people through the buying process.

Keep in mind that the blogosphere is not a used car lot, and overly pushy promotions can get negative comments from experienced blog readers and posters. Instead of nagging "buy now!" exclamations, we believe the best way to convert a visitor into a buyer is to simply make it easy for them to make a buying decision. Smart commerce-oriented bloggers utilize several techniques to help facilitate this process; here are a few key ideas.

Make it clear what you do, and the products you sell. A brief paragraph about your company containing a link to your product pages should be positioned near the top of your blog's home page.

Post about positive customer experiences. Testimonials from satisfied customers in the sidebars (again with links to products) can help visitors overcome any objections to buying that they might have. You can boost sales dramatically by researching why people are reluctant to buy your product and featuring customer comments directly refuting those common reasons. Mentioning products in posts and linking back to pages that allow purchasing also works well.

Leverage trusted commerce sites your visitors may rely on now. Many potential buyers are hesitant to provide credit card information to unfamiliar blogs, and prefer not to have to re-enter contact information. Clip-n-Seal uses at least two popular shopping cart systems that permit buying through services that have millions of registered users. Visitors can purchase through

PayPal (with more than 20 million account holders) or Amazon (with more than 40 million account holders). Other prominent services many bloggers use include Yahoo! and eBay.

The bottom line here is that blogs intended to sell products require frequent posts that describe product offerings and discuss how customers are successfully (or unexpectedly!) using these products. Posts should also contain direct links to buy. Think about posts with subjects like "Megacorp CEO says ACME industrial lubricant also makes an excellent dessert topping" or "Boeing saves an estimated three million dollars a year using ACME widgets."

Driving More Traffic to Your Current Web Site

Most of the businesspeople that have approached us with an interest in blogging already have a Web site and are very motivated to have more people visit it. Blogs have proven to be very effective at driving traffic to traditional sites, and many companies have made them a cornerstone of their promotional strategies.

37signals is a company that offers a set of Web-based applications that help businesses manage projects. Within the traditional site is their Signal vs. Noise blog, which, according to company president Jason Fried, "drives more traffic by far to our site than any other vehicle." Those 20,000 daily readers of the Signal vs. Noise blog also contribute more to the company's annual bottom line than all other advertising, direct mail, and email marketing campaigns combined.

If generating more sales is the major reason your business is considering blogging, there are a few things to consider right off the bat. One key decision to make early pertains to the domain where you want your blog to be hosted. You should seriously consider having it hosted under the same domain as your company site. For example, 37signals resides at: *www.37signals.com* and the Signal vs. Noise blog is at *www.37signals.com/svn/*. This location means that when visitors come to the blog, they are already within the confines of the main site, and any inbound links from people referencing the blog add Google juice to the main site as well. It's not unlike having a popular restaurant within a hotel. The more people who come to dine, the more visibility the entire facility will receive.

This arrangement is a bit more complex than just signing up for a Blogger, WordPress, or TypePad account. First of all, you'll want to contact the Web team that manages your current site, and see if they can enable this. Also, the easy and inexpensive hosted blog services generally can't host sub-domain blogs like this, so you'll want to consider a higher-end pro blogging tool like WordPress or Movable Type. We'll cover those options in greater depth in Chapter 4, "Designing for Readers."

You'll also want to put systems into place for tracking how many visitors enter the main site via the blog. Your Webmaster and technical team can use server logs information to help measure this. There are other tools available to help track visits that we'll discuss later in this chapter.

A Public Relations Focus

Do you work for a company that may have stumbled along the path to success? Perhaps your company has inadvertently shipped products containing technical glitches or other errors? Many image problems can be resolved or reduced by putting a "human face" on the organization, and one of the best ways to do that is to ask interesting and diplomatic employees to write about what they do and how much they care about satisfying customers.

Of course, you don't have to have an image problem to benefit from PR-focused blogging. For many companies—especially those that can't afford print, radio, or television advertising—a Web presence provides the "public face" of the business to customers and potential customers.

Dealing with Disasters

While your blog can serve as an ideal platform for writing about things that promote your company or products, it can also serve as an important channel in which to respond to negativity from others.

Several high-profile companies have experienced the wrath of angry bloggers because of product or service gaffes. CBS news, Sony BMG, Alaska Airlines, and Dell have all faced significant PR challenges due to how they responded (or didn't respond) to critical bloggers.

These companies discovered the hard way that detractors in the blogosphere can have significant influence over the mainstream press, and all faced front-page exposure of embarrassing problems due to their lack of blog-savviness.

In all of those examples, rather than post or comment in response to criticism, the companies stonewalled. This silence fed into the blogger's escalating speculation and accusations. In some cases, press releases were eventually issued, but it essentially amounted to wrong channel and bad timing.

The bottom line is you need to watch the bloggers closely and have people empowered to respond honestly and quickly to criticism. This may be a tall order for some organizations, but it's mandatory in this era of instant communications.

The blogosphere is very forgiving to companies that respond honestly and rapidly. In Chapter 7, we'll teach you more about how to monitor the blogosphere and specifically how to respond to bloggers and comments on your site(s).

Reputation and Recognition

IBM has effectively projected an image of smarts for decades. Their long-time motto of "Think" is even more relevant today as IBM's central focus is on consulting services. IBM has jumped into blogging, with over 11,000 public blogs up and running. Their intent is to have as many IBM bloggers as possible contributing to the commentary on the Web, and have now formally encouraged all of their 320,000 staff and executives to start posting.

Why would a huge multinational technology company want their people to take time away from their core duties to talk openly about their products, technologies, issues, and expertise? One key reason is to position IBM scientists, engineers, and staff as "thought leaders."

Thought leadership is a way of differentiating your company from others by being perceived as an organization where industry experts, innovators, and influencers converge. As Mike Wing, IBM's vice president of strategic communications said in an interview, "IBM is a company based on expertise and collaborative innovation—those are basically the company's business model."

Thought leadership is often the critical branding element organizations seek when they embrace blogging. In a 2005 survey of corporate bloggers by Backbone Media, 73 percent listed it as either the "primary reason" they blogged or as "very important."

IBM originally went public with a set of blogs hosted by a key developer relations group. The intent was to deliver support and insight to outside software programmers. This DeveloperWorks site (*www.ibm.com/developerworks*) is now hosting more than 20 blogs being read by many thousands of customers and partners daily.

These successes prompted IBM to create a set of blogging guidelines that would empower and encourage all employees to participate in the blogging initiative. In May 2005, they formally launched the companywide effort.

Many organizations working to foster a positive image have asked key employees to blog. If you are tempted to do the same, comprehensive policies and systems will need to be put into place, and careful monitoring of what's being said is mandatory.

Many thought leadership blogs are not intended to be read by direct customers or intended customers of a company, but are targeted instead toward influential people (often other bloggers and/or members of the press) with the hope that these readers will write about (and reinforce) what the thought leader is trying to project.

The bottom line for an image management blog is that you'll need to empower key employees to post (and respond to posts other bloggers make) frequently about topics that show how smart, innovative, and caring your company is. An example post subject line might be "We just submitted a new manufacturing process to the patent office for approval."

A Customer Focus

We know that blog technologies enable conversations, which not only help sell products, but also help take care of customers after they've purchased something.

Remember that a business blog is like a newsletter with interactivity. Thanks to comments, customers can interact with you in a more intimate way than a generic "contact us" form. Also, posts about your product can provide answers to commonly asked questions, or solutions to issues that have been raised previously.

A good example of a customer service blog is Kinkless GTD (*www.kinkless. com*), a project management application produced and distributed via a blog by Ethan J. A. Schoonover. Not only does his blog promote and distribute the software, but it also supports the people who use it. The user guide and online help are formed from blog posts, and readers supply supplemental information in the comments attached to those posts (**Figure 2.2**). If you have a question about how to use Kinkless GTD, you can search the blog and most likely find the answer right away. The customer focus on the Kinkless blog is building a community of users.

Figure 2.2

The Kinkless GTD project management application is supported exclusively by its blog. Customers can peruse the blog to find answers to frequently asked questions, or create a new comment and receive an answer from another customer.

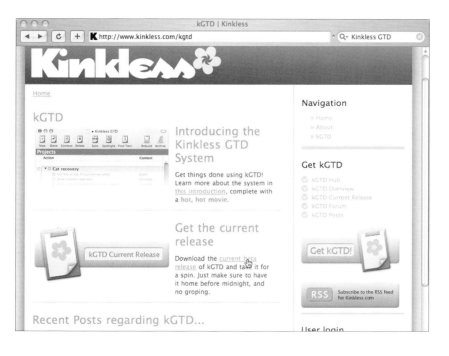

Paul Rosenfeld is the General Manager for QuickBooks Online Edition. He launched the QuickBooks Online Weblog (*www.quickbooksgroup.com*), another example of a customer service blog, in part to provide support for his customers. Many of the posts his group creates discuss how to get more out of the software and solve problems. The QuickBooks blog, shown in **Figure 2.3**, also presents customer success stories, and has a frequently updated list of links that can route visitors to other support resources, such as discussion groups.

Intuit tracks customer satisfaction scores for various divisions, and the QuickBooks Online Edition scores are among the highest in the company. Paul says their blog plays an important role in that success. In a post he wrote entitled "How we manage the business," Paul relayed how a QuickBooks customer posted this comment: "In the past I've been totally put off by Intuit's sealed lips policy about upcoming features in the desktop version. Paul Rosenfeld's customer inclusive approach is like a ray of sunshine."

Figure 2.3

The QuickBooks Online Weblog is one of the best options on the Web for QuickBooks Online support.

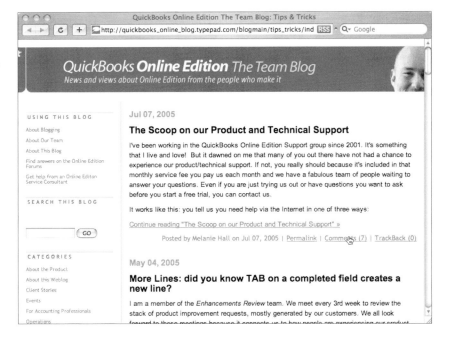

Measuring Success

After you've picked a focus for your blogging efforts and set goals for the initiative, how will you determine that you're succeeding (or not)? While it can be hard to quantify the general goodwill a blog generates, there are other measures available that can at least roughly determine how many people are paying attention to your efforts.

For most of the blog approaches discussed in this chapter, setting and monitoring benchmarks for traffic, mentions of you or your product on blogs, and/or inbound links will be helpful. Analyzing specific numbers for a competitor or partner's site or blog may serve as a starting point for setting the target numbers for your blog.

A simple goal could be to increase Google search results for the phrase "ACME Widget" to a specific number within a few months of your launch.

 TIP: Using quotation marks in the search will ensure that you don't find pages that talk about ACME Rocket Sled Corporation in Widget, Oklahoma.

Another very useful, yet only slightly more complex Google search is one that tracks inbound links. To see how many other pages Google finds that link back to your Web site, just enter the phrase "link:" just before the URL to your main domain. For example, if your home page is at *www.mybusiness.com*, you'd type *link: www.mybusiness.com* into the Google search box, and the number of inbound links will result (plus you can also see and visit those linking to you). In addition, you can go to Google's Advanced Search page and enter your URL into the Page-Specific Search area.

While Google tracks Web sites in general, Technorati is a search engine that exclusively tracks blogs and how they link to one another. The Top 100 Popular Blogs view shown in **Figure 2.4** is based on links to and from blogs. The blogs with the most links are the most popular. Tracking your Technorati ranking can also give you an idea of how well your blog is doing.

Figure 2.4

Bloggers use Technorati to discover what's going on in the blogosphere, where their site ranks, how many bloggers link to it, and the popularity of topics.

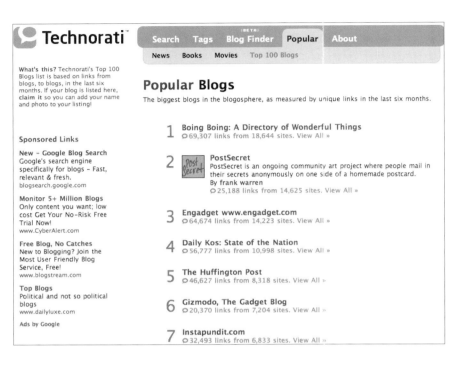

Server log data, which most Web site hosting services provide, can specifically track the number of visitors who come to your e-commerce site via your blog—and whether or not they purchase something. These reports are generated from programs such as Analog or Webalizer. Ask your host or Web management team about getting these reports. In addition, Google has begun to offer their useful Analytics site reports for free. The service, shown in **Figure 2.5**, offers a granular view of your blog traffic and reports on what your readers are doing when they come to the site. All you need to do to receive these Analytics reports is get a Google account and download a small bit of programming code that you paste into your home page.

While server log reports can tell you specifically how many people visit your Web site, they don't allow you to compare your blog traffic numbers to other sites (such as competitors' blogs). For that purpose, you should check out Alexa (*www.alexa.com*). Alexa tracks, shown in **Figure 2.6**, where people that have installed the Alexa toolbar application have been surfing, and can tell you how (at least for Alexa users) visits to your site compare to others.

Figure 2.5

Google Analytics offers free, powerful reporting features for your blog.

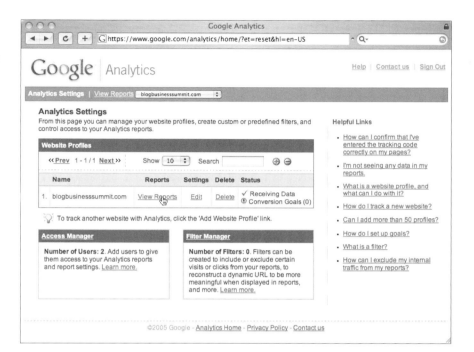

Figure 2.6

You can use Alexa to compare the popularity of two sites over a period of time. Alexa is good for quick comparisons, but note that traffic stats and traffic patterns are not an exact science.

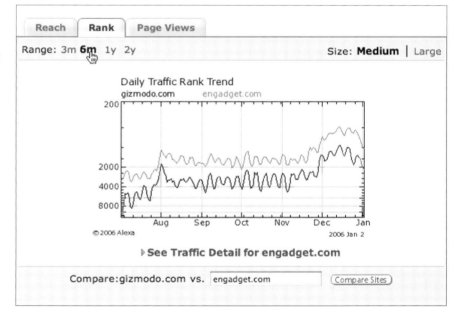

As you can see in the Alexa chart, Gizmodo, a popular gadget blog, is generally one of the top 1500 sites tracked, and Engadget, a competitor, appears to be more popular, ranking within the top 1000 sites.

 NOTE: One problem with measuring how many people visit your site is that you're not getting a reading on how many people are reading your content, thanks to syndication—that is, readers subscribing to your RSS feeds. We go into more detail on RSS in Chapter 5.

Before you launch any major blogging initiative, take the time to define what you hope to achieve by blogging and how you'll measure success. If you establish your goals in advance, you'll find it easier to decide what system to use, what to post about, and how to write.

Start Blogging Now

We've heard many successful bloggers tell businesspeople interested in blogging to "just jump in and start." At first glance these experts don't appear to be taking a careful and reasoned approach. Shouldn't they be advising people to gather data, research the arena, establish goals, and plan their execution? Isn't promoting the "jump in and start posting" philosophy a bit impulsive and perhaps even irresponsible?

It can certainly seem odd that experts will on the one hand promote the blogosphere as a sophisticated and powerful new medium (with the power to "destroy brands and wreck lives" according to the cover of *Forbes*) yet on the other hand appear to be saying "don't plan, just execute."

The advice to "start blogging now" is really quite consistent with a carefully thought-out and competently executed business blogging strategy. The experience gained from launching, designing, and posting to a simple "starter" blog is a critical component in the obligatory "data gathering" phase of developing an informed business blogging strategy.

The individuals involved in determining how a company may or may not blog should at least set up their own small-scale blogs and get a feel for what the process is like, and how the tools work.

In other words, you can't effectively plan until you have some relevant direct experience. Your company doesn't need to have an "official" blog yet, but key decision makers should at least open accounts and start posting about whatever strikes their fancy—their pets, favorite restaurants, or great business books they've read. These blogs don't even need to be publicly accessible at first. Many blog services allow for password-protected sites that even the search engines don't visit.

Learning to be a successful blogger is not unlike learning to be a good swimmer. Reading and listening to experts will only take you so far. You have to get into the pool, and the sooner the better! Once you splash around for a while in the shallow end and get a feel for things, then you can better understand how to swim in the deep end and keep your head above water. Eventually you can head out into the ocean and ride the waves.

The "just start blogging" strategy can seem like a major risk to most businesses. But if it feels like a stretch for you, consider this scenario:

You work for a huge company with deep layers of management and your public communications are restricted by SEC regulations and military security concerns. In that instance, you might find it almost impossible to launch a public blog written by a top executive. But as daunting as it sounds, this is exactly what Boeing did.

You Go Out, You Get Better

Chris Brownrigg, a top Web designer for Boeing, got the "blog call" from Commercial Airplanes Communications in early 2005. Boeing needed to address the press that its main competitor, Airbus, was receiving for the launch of its massive 800-seat passenger jet. Corporate communications had followed the blogs of other companies, like Sun and GM, and decided a blog might be just the thing. They told Chris he had two days to figure out how a blog worked, learn how to build it, and get it ready to publish. He used the traditional tools of the Web design trade to hand-build a "blog" site that was posted almost immediately.

Randy's Journal, penned by Randy Baseler—vice president of marketing for the Boeing Commercial Airplane Company—allowed Boeing to state its case and turn attention back to its own products.

Although the Boeing blog was a solid public relations win, it was initially criticized for its lack of usual blog features such as commenting, permalinks, RSS feeds, and related links. The early version is shown in **Figure 2.7**.

Figure. 2.7

The first version of Boeing's blog. Notice how it lacks a sidebar, and includes boeing.com's navigation elements and no search.

Boeing quickly realized that they needed to respond constructively to the criticism being offered up by the blogosphere. To do this, the architecture of the site itself had to be revamped, so Boeing hired Byron's company, Textura Design, to develop the next version of the site. (The more robust version is shown in **Figure 2.8**.)

This was an important step for Boeing. Not only were they able to effectively demonstrate their adaptability and sensitivity to the contributions of the blogosphere, they also got a crash course in responding effectively to criticism.

Savvy readers received the new version warmly, and the blog now attracts more traffic and places much higher in Google searches than did the first version of the blog.

Boeing's blog is an example of how strategy and planning can happen after a blog has launched. There's an old dotcom saying, "you go out, you get better," and Boeing proved that you could do just that.

Figure 2.8

Boeing's revised blog after the company considered initial reader feedback. They added a sidebar with a calendar, a search function, and its own navigation, independent of www.boeing.com.

ACT FIRST, PLAN LATER: THE GOOGLE SUCCESS STORY

Scared to blog before you've fully planned your strategy? Big business rarely takes the approach business guru Tom Peters likes to call "Ready. Fire. Aim." Instead, most managers pursue the tried-and-true scenario of: Gather data, plan, get consensus, then execute.

One notable company that departed from the conventional model is Google. Few people realize that as late as 2001 (at least two years after the company received funding), Google's founders had still not yet figured out how the business was going to make money. The decision to host ads came only after dozens of other potential ideas had been rejected.

Considering Google dedicated millions of dollars and years of effort toward building a winning search engine before focusing on a business model, you can feel relatively guilt-free for spending a few dollars and a few hours posting before you have to create the perfect blog solution for your company.

Although Boeing didn't get everything right the first time, it was a good initial effort, and the company responded quickly with appropriate changes. It proved that even big companies with an entrenched communications infrastructure could effectively launch, learn, and adapt. In fact, Boeing's first blog was so successful they launched another for the flight test of the 777-200LR and have more planned.

The key points here: no staging, no stakeholder meetings, no flowcharting, and no architecture diagrams. Boeing just started blogging.

Reading this book and talking to experienced bloggers will certainly help you find success in the blogosphere, but the single most important move you can make is to log into Blogger or one of the other free services and set up a test blog for yourself. In fact, we're advising you to do that right now—it's simple and will only take a few minutes. You'll get even more out of this book with that experience under your belt. Go ahead and sign up now. We'll wait while you post about this book and how great your blog is going to be. In the next chapter, you'll learn what resources you're going to need to make your blog a success.

Chapter 3

How Much Blog— and How Often?

If you've taken our advice and have fired up a "starter" blog, you've got a taste of what's required of you and your team to maintain at least a minimal presence in the blogosphere. As you are likely aware by now, blogging is fairly simple—but it's not effortless.

As many potential bloggers have learned the hard way, a blog without the resources to support it can turn a good idea into an embarrassing situation. A 2004 survey by Perseus Development Corporation found that 66 percent of surveyed blogs had not been updated in two months, making almost three million blogs that had been for all practical purposes abandoned. If you want your blog(s) to avoid this fate, make sure your company's resources and cultures align.

In this chapter, we'll cover the resource needs that business bloggers will want to consider, and how to rally the troops behind a blogging initiative.

What's It Going to Take?

As with many business initiatives, there's some circular logic that needs to be dealt with in the early stages of blog planning. The chicken-and-egg situation is that you can't easily ask for specific company resources when launching a business blog until you know what you need, yet you don't want to initiate extensive planning on a campaign unless you have an idea of what assets are available.

Fortunately, with a blogging initiative, there are two factors in play that make life much easier for you as you start to plan. One is that you don't need to launch an expensive and labor-intensive project to get many of the benefits of blogging. Even a simple and inexpensive presence in the blogosphere can reap dividends.

Another factor is that growing a very small blog initiative into something bigger is relatively straightforward. An organization can apply more resources to a blog (or series of blogs) to grow the presence and audience without facing significant growing pains. In other words, blogging is not like manufacturing hard goods; you don't need to buy land, build a new factory, and get showroom space to expand your operations.

In Chapter 1, "Meet the Blogs," we described a spectrum of business blogging approaches available to you. These included a couple of very low-risk options that don't require any employees to actually blog. In this chapter, we'll focus on the alternatives that will require team members to be actively involved in posting and maintaining a business blogging presence. We'll describe what levels of cost and time commitment would be required to put each into action.

Once we've laid out the scenarios, you can factor in what's realistic for your organization, and make a plan of action.

A Basic Blog

At the most basic level, you can set up a minimal presence with a free or inexpensive blog account on a hosted service like Blogger, TypePad, or Blog Harbor and have someone post as little as three to four times a week. While you can post less often than this, remember that search engines factor in frequency of updates when ranking results—so it's best to do what you can to post more often.

Part of this obligation should include time spent monitoring what other bloggers might be saying about your business and responding to their posts or comments. We'll cover this more thoroughly in Chapter 8, "Monitoring and Managing Your Blog."

The cash requirements for such a low-effort blog would be at most $25 per month for a subscription to a hosted service, and you should reasonably budget for someone to spend four to five hours a week to maintain this minimal presence. Expect to dedicate 20 hours or so to launching the blog and mastering the initial learning curve.

A starter level blog can be run by a single trusted individual who has the knowledge and judgment to make intelligent posts and won't likely expose the organization to any legal liabilities or embarrassment. While it's best to always have formal blogging policies in place, many of the businesses that have deployed a single trusted part-time blogger have not established formal rules, and instead have an informal "use your best judgment" standard. For example, the managers at Internet telephony provider Skype know that their employees are going to use their best judgment when posting to the company blog, Share Skype (*www.share.skype.com/sites/en*). The blog, started as a way for employees to share what they think is cool about the product, the company, and the user community, is low-budget, low-effort, and lots of fun for both Skype employees and customers (**Figure 3.1**).

Figure 3.1

Share Skype builds a community between Skype employees and their customers.

A Full-Time Blog

To pursue an expanded presence, some companies have established either a single "full-time" blog or multiple "part-time" blogs in hopes of achieving a higher level of benefits. Both scenarios require significantly more time and effort than the basic level, but can reap big rewards. For a full-time blog, you might have one dedicated person involved, or a team of people contributing to the site.

The QuickBooks Online Weblog is an example of a single blog with a team of contributors, and IBM's developerWorks blogs typify a group of individual writers contributing to their own individual blogs under a corporate umbrella.

In either plan, many more total posts a week will be written, and more planning is required. In this scenario, you'd almost certainly want to graduate from a free blogging service to a paid one with more features, and one that can allow for multiple blogs to be hosted from a single user account.

For a multiple blog scenario, it's most likely best to host the blogs on your own servers (which we'll cover in more depth in Chapter 5, "Tools and Implementation"). Implementation will primarily depend on the availability of technical staff or the money available to fund blog-savvy consultants.

It's likely that for this more comprehensive scenario, a formal blogging policy would be put into place. Plan on potentially dozens of hours and several meetings to establish an appropriate policy for your needs. (For more specifics on policies, see the sidebar "Establishing Guidelines and Policies," later.)

The primary cost for this level is staff time spent posting, along with reading others' posts and responding to comments, general planning, and establishing policies.

It's conceivable that at this level of commitment an organization that executes well would over time gain a very healthy level of Google juice, and a nontrivial amount of mindshare from other prominent bloggers. Microsoft's Robert Scoble, who we consider to be a "full-time" blogger, gets tens of thousands of influential visitors a day thanks to his efforts, and Google places his posts prominently in search results.

A Sponsored Blog

Instead of launching their own full-time blogs, companies like Connexion by Boeing, Sony, and McDonald's have all tried out the blogosphere by sponsoring blogs. As we discussed in Chapter 1, the inFlightHQ blog has been very successful for Connexion by Boeing. They're reaching the business traveler demographic and relying upon the expertise of the bloggers to do so. This "blog without blogging" effort will require coordination between your company, the blog publishers, and an ad agency. If you sign up to sponsor a blog, you'll want specific metrics and traffic results to measure the success. The companies we know, like Connexion, have found that sponsoring a blog is a great way to try out their brand in the blogosphere and see how well blogging works for them.

A Companywide Blog

Some ambitious companies have taken the ultimate plunge and are empowering all employees to blog. Sun Microsystems is one of these organizations and has encouraged their 35,000 employees to share their work with the world without asking permission.

So far, 1000 employees have started blogging, and Sun has built a custom system to manage these employee sites.

Naturally, Sun has spent a great deal of time and effort creating a culture and set of guidelines that minimizes the risks of inappropriately posted information being put out for the world to see.

If you work for a large company like Sun, launching and maintaining this kind of comprehensive blogging campaign will almost certainly mean installing a dedicated hosting system, and requires allocating significant technical staff hours to monitor and manage the hardware and software that enables it. Conceivably, the direct expenses can range into tens of thousands of dollars annually.

Potentially the biggest cost to an employer is the loss of employee productivity as they focus precious time on blogging. Naturally, no company wants their employees to spend all of their time writing about their work; they'd rather just have them *doing* the work.

Sun has a policy that addresses this. Sun's position is that while they don't limit the amount of time an employee uses to blog, they do expect a blogging employee's workload to remain unchanged.

ESTABLISHING GUIDELINES AND POLICIES

One resource consideration you'll need to factor in is the need to dedicate some time with your team to decide what your company policies will be toward blogging. Some companies that blog don't institute a formal policy and it's certainly easiest not to draft one, but you'll at least want to be clear about what's expected from your bloggers.

Establishing guidelines is a pretty straightforward process. Fortunately, other companies have already done much of the groundwork for you. Many existing policies are available online to review, and experience demonstrates that even a bare bones policy can go a long way toward minimizing problems.

While Microsoft does not have an official policy regarding employee blogging, many of the bloggers agree that the unofficial guideline is simply "don't be stupid." Similarly, for some time Sun's blogging policy was simply "don't make forward-looking statements"—in other words, don't post about how next quarter's financials are shaping up.

You'll want to go online and look up some of the policies that are out there for review. Sun, IBM, Harvard Law School, and many other organizations have posted their rules for anyone to look at. In some cases, they've even documented how they reached those policies.

Some common rules to consider are:

- Identify yourself when posting. Make it clear on the blog who you are and what your role is at the company.

- Employees should make it known that the views expressed in the blog are theirs alone and do not necessarily represent the views of the employer.

- Write with respect toward the company, other employees, customers, partners, and competitors.

- Don't reveal any confidential or proprietary information.

- Don't let time spent blogging interfere with your work responsibilities.

- Employees must comply with other company policies, and rules outlined in the company handbook(s).

- Direct all press inquires to your manager or the corporate communications department.

- When in doubt, ask your manager.

To read some of these policies, see the Corporate Blogging Wiki (*www.socialtext.net/bizblogs/*).

Assessing Resources, Barriers, and Culture

Compared to other marketing and communications initiatives with world-wide reach, it doesn't take much to launch and maintain a successful business blog. You'll need to bring to the table your goals, a small team with a little time, good ideas for content, and the support of your organization.

Take some time to inventory what assets are available to you, and determine whether or not they are adequate to get the job done. The specifics of what you'll need are detailed below.

Regular and Ongoing Posting

A blog without posts is like a city without buildings—there isn't a whole lot of motivation to visit, and not much to see when you get there. For public sites, readers (and search engines!) need a reason to drop by. Multiple posts are that reason. If contributors aren't making frequent and interesting contributions to the site, you'll find much of the oft-touted benefits of blogging evaporate.

While the most important thing is to write posts that are relevant to your audience, it's also vital that you do it frequently enough that search engines see the blog as an actively updated site and your readers have a reason to come back.

The topic of how often is enough is actively discussed in the blogosphere, and there are differing opinions. Based on discussions with various bloggers receiving significant traffic, our opinion is that three posts a week is a nice minimum to target and three a day is what can get you into the big leagues.

Staff Availability and Dedication

Posting is essential, and posting means people. People with the time, energy, and desire to write about relevant subjects. Luckily, we're not talking about a huge commitment here. Many successful blogs thrive with just a single passionate individual working only a few hours a day. Are you that person? Do you have people on staff (or who can be contracted) to contribute? We believe that most high-profile marketing-related blogs need at least two good hours a day of effort to stay viable, and highly recommend that a team be formally assembled to ensure those hours will be put in before any public launch of a blog.

Be aware that in our experience the vast majority of good-intentioned "volunteer posters" who say they are "happy to help out" and will post won't ever find the time. Have the commitment from contributors in writing, and have a designated manager or editor make sure posters are fulfilling their obligations. If the commitment and corporate buy-in are great enough, consider paying someone extra for their blogging or hiring a person just to blog.

Culture of Openness

Most of the companies known for having great success in the blogosphere have a culture of openness and transparency. These companies generally lean toward permitting "outsiders" to observe their operations—where practical—and even provide input. Open companies tend to let people see what they do and discuss themselves more openly.

With regard to blogging, Microsoft has a culture of openness. The company has embraced blogging as an important tool for reaching out to software developers, customers, and other partners. Microsoft now publishes over a thousand blogs on topics ranging from their new operating system to the minutiae of Internet Explorer's font rendering. Many of these blogs contain references to upcoming products and even tout opinions that differ with stated company positions.

While we believe that almost all companies can and should blog, it's clear that many of the corporate blogs we see today just won't work in many organizations. For those companies, the stereotypical employee or executive blog containing posts discussing projects the author is working on just won't cut it. In addition, openly accepting comments from outsiders critical of the company or their products is inconceivable to many managers.

With this in mind, one should gauge quickly how "open" their company might be to a dialog-style blog and reject the idea if the organization generally has a "loose lips sink ships" mindset. If your company is like Apple—

who carefully guard their secrets (and send lawyers after bloggers who reveal them!)—you just can't blog the same way Sun or Microsoft does.

If you determine that you have a fairly closed culture, it does not mean blogging is impossible. There are many good options available to you. Even the tightly constricted Apple culture has enabled successful blogs, and you can use that as a potential model for your efforts.

One of Apple's blogs (*http://education.apple.com/students/blog/*), shown in **Figure 3.2,** is for students with posts about campus life and using Apple products. The Apple Student Blog is about community, not about their corporation or Steve Jobs. Apple has also embraced blog-related technologies, like RSS. They have feeds available on most every page on their site, including technical note updates, Help files, and support forums available for subscription. Apple also publishes another blog about their .Mac service, which includes entries about how to best use the service. Apple is blogging in a manner that works for them and their culture.

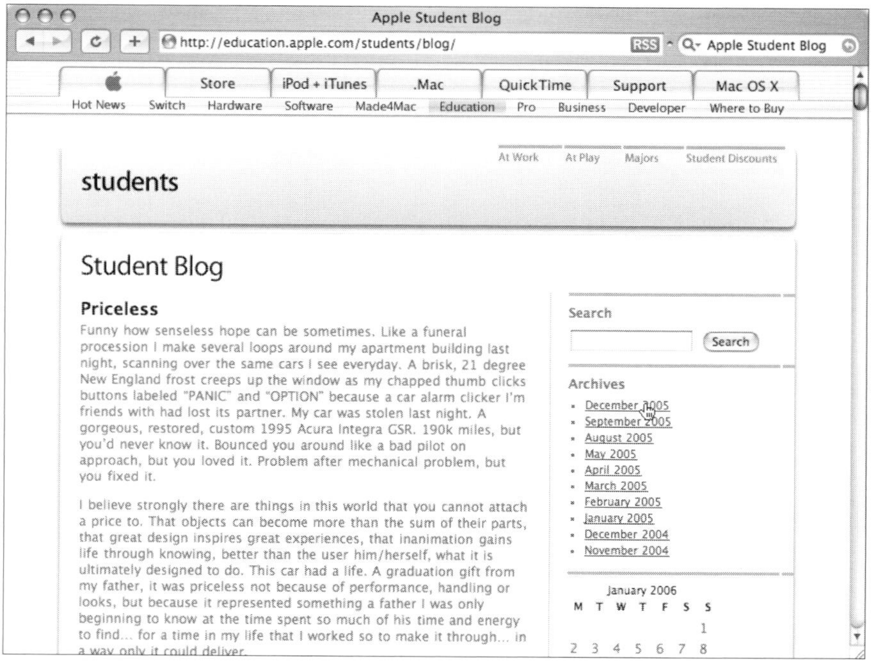

Figure 3.2

Apple's blog is for the college lifestyle and discusses Apple's products. The key here is to plan and promote a realistic blog initiative that makes sense given the culture you have.

Financial Resources

While it's true that the hardware and software requirements to successfully run any single blog are minimal, maintaining a truly popular blog can become nearly a full-time job depending on the number of posts required, and the effort one wants to put in on monitoring comments. In other words, the time and opportunity costs can be significant.

In addition, those circumstances in which companies encourage all of their employees to blog may require the licensing of many copies of software or large-scale subscription costs.

Do your homework before picking a platform, and make sure you've factored in all costs. We'll get more specific about software and pricing in Chapter 5.

Fostering Corporate Buy-In

It's no secret that fear is a strong motivator (or de-motivator). In 2005, a survey of senior marketers indicated that "fear of losing control of the company message" and "worries about what employees would write" were two of the most-often cited reasons that companies had not launched a blogging initiative.

These fears do have some foundation. Google, Delta Airlines, Microsoft, and a handful of other companies have indeed fired irresponsible bloggers who had posted information that was confidential or proved embarrassing to the organizations they worked for. Of course, these few high-profile cases stand in stark contrast to the millions of bloggers who post regularly about employer-related issues without compromising the companies they work for.

There are risks, no doubt about it, yet based on the statistics and our personal experience, we know that these risks can be largely mitigated through clear policies and diligent monitoring and feedback.

It's not unlike commercial jet travel. Strapping yourself into an aluminum tube and then letting the ignition of flammable gases propel you six miles up into the air could also sound a bit risky to the uninitiated. Combine that with the hope that the tube finds and gently descends to a perfect alignment on a narrow strip of pavement thousands of miles away, and it all sounds pretty crazy.

It's counterintuitive, but thanks to careful planning and engineering, flying is one of the safest things you can do. So is blogging—if you have the right people and the right game plan. The challenge is getting the fearful to understand so the process can begin.

Here are a couple tips that will assist you in your efforts to promote greater understanding of the safety and benefits of blogging.

BLOGOSPHERE DEFINITION

Dooced *(v.)* — To lose your job because of your blog.

The term was coined after blogger Heather Armstrong, whose blog is called Dooce (*www.dooce.com/*), was fired in 2002 for her postings about her coworkers. Since then, others have been fired, including a Google employee and a flight attendant. In those cases, the blogger blogged what they shouldn't have, forgetting that the rules in the workplace are more rigid than the blogosphere.

Get a Champion

If you research the stories and case studies surrounding the initiation of blogs in various businesses, you'll discover that often a lone senior executive was the driver behind getting a blog launched. In Boeing's case, the driver was Randy Baseler, vice president of marketing for Boeing Commercial Airplanes. For Stonyfield Farms, it was CEO Gary Hirshberg.

Consider targeting executives that have a leaning toward "guerrilla marketing" strategies. We've discovered that those who pursue word-of-mouth and other grassroots methods of creative promotion are more inclined to embrace blogging. Print or email the many articles in *The Wall Street Journal, Fortune, Business Week,* and *The Financial Times* that reinforce blogs as an effective and inexpensive promotional platform. Google your competitors that are blogging, and show how they're using blogs and where they place in search results.

One persuasive approach is to compare traffic trends of traditional sites versus their blog counterparts. Using Alexa charts to depict traffic patterns of sites your potential champion is familiar with, you can demonstrate how quickly blog traffic can match or eclipse their old-school equivalents.

Even when you have an influential champion working the problem, you can still expect some resistance. Christine Halvorson, Chief Blogger for Stonyfield Farms (The Bovine Bugle blog, shown in **Figure 3.3**), said at a blogging conference in 2005 that it was no slam-dunk for CEO Hirshberg to institute blogging. He had to convince reluctant marketing and PR teams that blogging was a good idea and it was going to be worth the company's effort. As it turns out, Hirshberg was right. Stonyfield's sales increased 25 percent over the last year, and has 750,000 subscribers to their "Moos Letters," a newsletter subscription service offered on their blogs.

Figure 3.3

Stonyfield's The Bovine Bugle blog (*www.stonyfield.com/ weblog/BovineBugle*) offers updates from their organic dairy farm in Franklin, Vermont. Past posts include weather reports, factoids about the cows, and birth announcements.

Simple Sells

Management guru Peter Drucker once said "effective innovations start small," and we think corporate blogs are a classic example of an advancement that fits this profile. Starting with a less-ambitious project is not only easier; it's also more likely to be approved.

The general rule is that once an organization starts a simple blogging effort and they begin to see the rewards, they're inclined to expand the program. This has been our anecdotal experience, and one that is also backed up by other statistics. The 2005 Guidewire Group survey of corporate blogging asked 5000 readers of *CMO Magazine* to respond to questions about their blogging activities. According to Guidewire: "No respondent reported launching a blog initiative that was found to be unsuccessful" and "No respondent plans to scale back or stop activity."

More proof of this comes from Stonyfield's Halvorson when she discussed the results of their initial blogging efforts with *BusinessWeek* for their May 2, 2005 story, "Stonyfield Farm's Blog Culture." The marketing and PR people "didn't know what a blog was," she says. "They were wary about what I was going to be saying that wasn't in their control. That was a year and a half ago."

Later in the year, Christine was on a blogging for business panel at the BlogHer 2005 conference and told the audience that "I was at a brainstorming meeting with these folks last week, where we plan what we're doing for the next year. By the end of the day, if I had a dime for every time I heard 'well, we oughta start a blog about that,' I'd be a rich woman. They all get it now."

With this in mind, consider what we advocated in Chapter 2, "Determining Your Focus." Propose a small, low-risk "starter" blog. If you can launch a blog that wins approval and then document the results, you stand a good chance of eventually expanding the project into something more comprehensive. Boeing launched another blog, and plans to launch more, because of the success of Randy's Journal.

To figure out how much time, energy, and money will be required to launch and maintain various blog strategies, you're going to need to do your homework. If you've got a good picture of what's going to be required and how the project can expand, you will be more likely to receive company resources. You'll also be able to better allocate those resources when you do get them.

In the next chapter, we'll help you understand what blog features are optimal for your mission, so that you can ultimately design a blog that fits your needs and budget.

Chapter 4

Designing for Readers

Blogs were born out of a minimalist approach to Web publishing and that same aesthetic can be found in their design. When blogs were first designed, way back in 1997, they were designed for content and little else. The early bloggers were less concerned with complicated layouts and menu systems, and more interested in talking to their friends and colleagues online. Blogs offered refreshing conversations with a light, airy approach to design that wasn't constrained by the demands of marketing, public relations, venture capitalists, and whole teams of sales people.

The blog aesthetic continues today, even with businesses, which find that a more casual design can effectively carry their messages.

In this chapter, we'll discuss how the right features, along with structural and visual design choices, allow you to develop a richer conversation with your readers. We'll also show you how to make good design choices by concentrating on simplicity and ease of use.

Essential Features

No matter what type of blog you are developing, there are core features you'll want to make available to the people who visit. These essential items will help you gain more visibility and ensure that your visitors can find everything they're looking for.

FEATURES AFFECT DESIGN

Good blog design focuses on providing useful content to visitors in a format that they can navigate easily. Readers want to understand very quickly who you are and what you have to say. They want to read recent posts, comment if they can, check your archives for other interesting information, link to your posts, and get your RSS feed. They don't expect to be confronted with complex menu systems or a Flash movie demo of your latest doodad.

Even though more and more Web sites today include multimedia features, many studies strongly suggest that people surfing the Web are not interested in animated interactive gadgetry. In 2003, the Pew Internet & American Life Project conducted a survey of several thousand Internet users and concluded that Web surfers are focused on looking for answers to specific questions, or are gathering research about products and services when they go online. Therefore, it's a smart move to focus on providing quality information. Anything that doesn't contribute directly to that end is best eliminated.

NOTE: The features that we will discuss in this chapter are available in somewhat different forms in all of the major blogging software. We'll go into the different software options available to you in Chapter 5, "Tools and Implementation."

Meta Information

Bloggers who review their visitor activity logs usually discover that their "About" page is one of the more frequently visited destinations on their sites. If people find your blog interesting, many will want to know more about you and your blog. This information is "data about data" and is frequently called *metadata*, or *meta* for short.

Practically all of the major blog engines provide a way for authors to include personal, professional, and contact information along with a photo on a dedicated page that is linked to prominently from the blog's home page. **Figure 4.1** shows an example of an About page. We highly recommend that you take advantage of this feature and make sure that this link is visible. We omitted this information on one of our first blogs and quickly started seeing comments from readers who were prompting us to include it.

Figure 4.1

Ben Goodger (*www.bengoodger.com*) is the Lead Engineer for Firefox. His About page is similar to a resume, listing his history, interests, and hobbies.

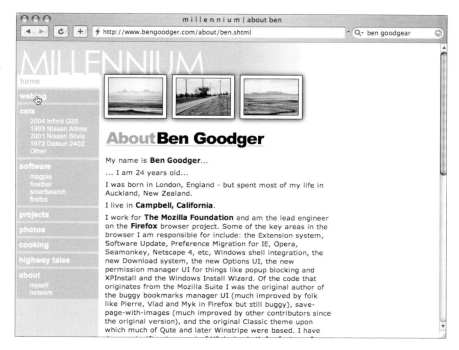

Jeremy Wagstaff is a technology columnist for the BBC and the *Wall Street Journal Online Edition* and publishes a personal blog called Loose Wire. Jeremy offers a considerable amount of data about himself and his blog (*www.loosewire.typepad.com*) in a sidebar.

We asked him why he is so open with personal information and he said, "As a traditional journalist we prided ourselves on limited accessibility. Give your name card out only to people who could be sources, not readers. It was one-way traffic and blogging has changed all of that. Now a reader is a source." Jeremy's approach to blogging is to be as accessible as possible and embrace the reader. Sharing all of that data is part of the conversation Jeremy has with his readers and the blogosphere.

Other examples of essential "About" information can be seen in **Figure 4.2** and **Figure 4.3**.

Your *sidebars,* meaning the column or columns that hold metadata, are valuable real estate. Taking a look at some established blogs will give you an idea of what sort of content generally goes in that space. In addition to your About page, other information you can provide includes lists of sites that link to you, maps of your business locations, recent comments, and traffic information. The blogosphere expects a certain amount of metadata on your site, and by offering it to them you're showing an openness to share information.

A list of links of interest to you, called a *blogroll*, is an important feature because it not only shows your readers what blogs you read, but it also indicates to search engines your relationship to other blogs. By linking to other blogs, you're connected to the blogosphere; as we've mentioned, search engines partly base page rank on the amount of links to and from a blog. Blogrolls are so popular that Web services like del.icio.us (*www.del.icio.us*), have been developed just to manage all the links.

You'll notice that sidebars also include things like your most recent posts, listed by title in chronological order. This is one of the ways that your blog posts can be organized, and we'll go into those next.

Organizing Entries

Quite often, you will be receiving first-time visits from people who have discovered one of your posts as a result of a search engine query. If you want to encourage these visitors to stick around for a while, you should make it easy for them to find additional posts they might like. If new visitors discover that your site is a treasure trove of information relevant to them, not only will they come back more often, but they might also subscribe to your feeds or ask to receive email updates.

Figure 4.2

Molly Holzschlag (*www.molly.com*) is an instructor, developer, and author of more than 30 books about the Web. She shares considerable information about herself and what she's doing in the blog sidebars. Also note that she places the About statement front and center.

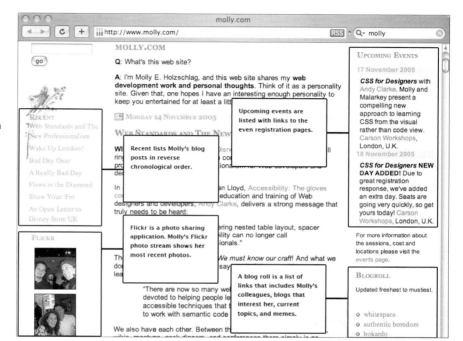

Figure 4.3

Fuji Film publishes a blog (*www.blimp.fujifilm.com*) about their blimp and includes personal picks from the Captain in the sidebar. They also encourage readers to contact the pilots with questions and send in their pictures. Fuji is creating a community around the blimp, a very visual part of their brand.

Knowing how blogs manage the storage and recall of posts (old and new) can help you better understand the options available to your readers for accessing them.

When new posts are created, the most recent post appears at the top of the blog home page, and older ones are pushed downward in chronological order. The page will only hold a certain amount of text; eventually, posts will be pushed off the page.

Luckily, these "banished" posts are still readily available to your visitors. Your blog software can automatically create a variety of archive pages on demand that contain all of your old posts, even those that no longer appear on the home page.

Because blogs are database-driven sites, each blog entry is assigned a unique record and a single permalinked "page" in a central database program. Think of every blog post you make as a single 3-by-5-inch card that is permanently stored in a filing box and retrievable, unless you delete it. Then imagine that copies of this card (or sets of cards) can be assembled and presented upon demand as visitors request them. This approach enables great flexibility in how posts can be grouped, compiled, and presented to your readers.

Categories

One of the handiest ways for old posts to be accessed is via category links. Blog software allows authors to create and assign one or more categories to their posts. The blog engine can then list all of the categories used in the sidebar. When one of the category links is clicked on, the blog software automatically gathers all posts in that specific category and presents them. Let's say you've written 100 posts over the past year, and you've categorized 20 of them under the heading "widget technologies." Most blog software will automatically put a "widget technologies" link in your sidebar, and when clicked, it will present a custom page showing all 20 posts that fit that category.

The fact that an original post is stored in the same place and is easily accessible *(permalinked)* also means that search engines that index your site will always know where to find any post you've written—even years after you've written it.

Recent Entries

Another set of automatically generated links that we recommend you put on your sidebar are links to recent entries. Business Logs, shown in **Figure 4.4,** is a blog that functions like an office water cooler with ongoing discussions about business blogging. The blog prominently features recent entries in the sidebar and uses a combination of visual design and copywriting to orient the reader very quickly.

Figure 4.4

Business Logs (*www. businesslogs.com*), as the name suggests, is a business blog whose posts are like team meetings in public. They post about topics they'd discuss in a meeting, and readers are invited to join the conversation and offer their opinions.

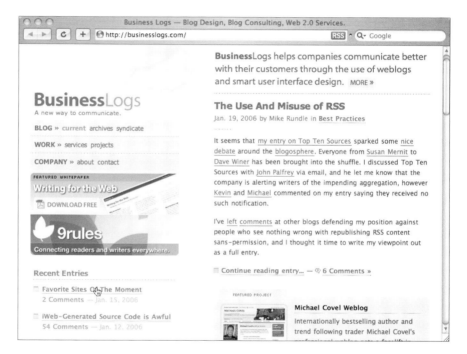

Remember that your blog is really a fun little CMS just publishing its heart out, and once those entries are in the database it'll happily display them in all sorts of ways. Bloggers will often show the most-commented and most-active posts in their sidebars. They'll also sometimes show how many posts are in a specific category, allow voting on how good a post is, and offer a quick form to email a post to a friend.

Tags

Another popular way to organize posts is called *tagging*. Unlike the standard category style described above (for example, "Action Movie Reviews"), tags are like ad-hoc categories based on keywords you can create anytime. You can apply as many tags as you want to any one post. For example, tags applied to an action movie review might be "Movies," "Schwarzenegger," and/or "Explosions."

Bloggers use tags to easily remember and recall topics in the posts they write. You've seen how categories are usually listed as clickable links in a sidebar, and tags can be displayed this way as well. Tags you've applied can be displayed as a *tag cloud*, which is a visual depiction of all current content tags in use. Tags are visually weighted in a tag cloud to indicate frequency of use, as shown in **Figure 4.5.**

Figure 4.5

Tags are searchable keywords that can be viewed in a tag cloud. On blogs like the Blog Business Summit and Union Square Ventures (*www. unionsquareventures. com*), tags are created by the post authors. On a social site like Flickr, where users share photos, the tags are created by the users.

![Flickr all time most popular tags cloud]

All time most popular tags — flickr

amsterdam animal animals april architecture art australia baby barcelona beach berlin bird birthday black blackandwhite blue boston bridge building bw california cameraphone camping canada car cat cats chicago china christmas church city clouds color colorado concert day dc dog dogs england europe family festival fireworks florida flower flowers food france friends fun garden geotagged germany girl graduation graffiti green hawaii holiday home honeymoon house india ireland italy japan july june kids lake landscape light london losangeles macro march may me mexico moblog mountains museum music nature new newyork newyorkcity newzealand night nyc ocean orange oregon paris park party people phone photo pink portrait red reflection river roadtrip rock rome sanfrancisco school scotland sea seattle sign sky snow spain spring street summer sun sunset taiwan texas thailand tokyo toronto travel tree trees trip uk unfound urban usa vacation vancouver washington water wedding white winter yellow zoo

NOTE: All blog systems let you establish and use categories, but many do not yet offer tagging as a standard feature. Some third-party tagging programs have become available and can be "plugged-in" to blog engines in order to add this function.

You should take advantage of categorical and chronological archives that make sense for your audience. Including these links in your sidebars will make your content more accessible to your visitors.

RSS and Syndication

One of the most compelling reasons to blog is provided by the integrated syndication options that blogs offer to authors and readers. Every time you post to your blog, it's possible to "broadcast" that entry worldwide to an audience of subscribers potentially numbering in the millions. All of the major blog software providers and hosting services have integrated this feed-broadcasting capability as a standard feature. Unless you are purposely trying to minimize the audience for your content, this is an option you'll definitely want to turn on and place prominently.

But what exactly is feed syndication, and how does it work?

Do you have several Web sites that you like to keep track of, but don't want to have to surf to those sites everyday and pick out just the new material? Wouldn't it be great if you could just scan a central "dashboard" that lists only the newest additions to a list of favorite sites? Others have had the same idea. In the mid-1990s, there was a lot of enthusiasm for this notion, and several companies offered products that promised "dashboard" programs like this.

While none of these first-generation products made much of an impact, a viable solution eventually came along. The sequential nature of blogging renewed the need for this sort of software. Several years ago, a new type of software for viewing Web content became popular among those who wanted to stay on top of the latest news and know when their favorite sites were updated. These programs, called newsreaders, receive "what's new" content from Web sites that support them. Like email programs, newsreaders list subject lines (headlines); when the user clicks on a headline, they can read the rest of the "message." These "messages" are really nothing more than snippets of new information that had just been put up on a Web site and broadcast via (you guessed it) RSS.

RSS stands for *Really Simple Syndication*. When a Web site is built to support syndication, newsreader software—like NetNewsWire, shown in **Figure 4.6**—and newsreader sites can subscribe to syndicated sites (usually for free) and receive the latest updates as soon as they happen.

Figure 4.6

The newsreader NetNewsWire is just one of many programs that allows you to view posts fed in from several different Web sites.

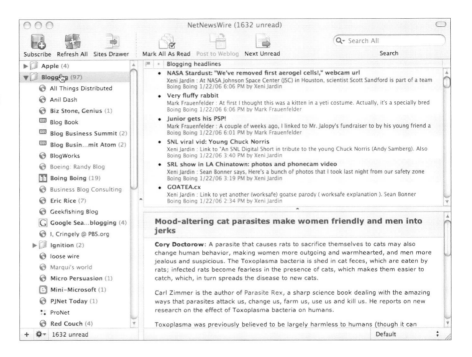

It took a few years, but syndication has caught on. Current counts indicate that 75 million people rely on newsreaders for information. Both Microsoft and Apple have incorporated news reading capabilities into their latest Web browsers and operating systems and it's built right into the Firefox browser. Many Web sites report that they now have more people reading their articles through newsreader programs than from direct visits to the site itself. Portal sites like MyYahoo! and the personalized version of Google offer RSS feed viewing as a content option that can be added to a headline section of the page. Bloglines is a Web-based service that aggregates and personalizes RSS feeds. It works very much like MyYahoo!, but just for RSS.

RSS AND TRAFFIC

One problem with RSS is that you don't get reliable statistics on how many people are reading your content. Getting that specific figure can be difficult, as the Web does not yet provide a mechanism to reliably track RSS subscriptions. It's possible that one single subscription is being re-fed to many readers, and it also may be that thousands are receiving your feeds yet not actually reading the posts contained within them.

A service called Feedburner provides a way for bloggers to offer subscription feeds that are far more measurable than standard RSS. In essence, they send out your feeds and then provide detailed reports about how your posts are being circulated. The system works well, but some bloggers don't like the fact that a third-party is managing the distribution of their content.

Subscribing to Feeds

How do you know if a site broadcasts feeds? It's easy—just look for the little orange button that says "RSS," "XML," or sometimes "Atom." If you see that button, you know that the site generates feeds. Other clues include the words "syndicate this site" as a link.

The act of subscribing is easy. The latest and greatest Web browsers like Firefox, Apple's Safari, or Internet Explorer version 7 can auto-detect that a site has an RSS feed and will automatically activate a clickable button in the browser that will start the subscription. For many of the programs that read feeds, you can drag that button or link into the newsreader application and voila! You are subscribed. Many people rely on the tried-and-true method of right-clicking on a subscription link to copy it, and then pasting the link into their newsreader as a new subscription.

Smart blog designers make this link, or an RSS button, prominent and place it near the top of their pages or the sidebars.

 NOTE: RSS and Atom are syndication formats based on XML. All major newsreaders should read them both and utilize the slightly different set of features each provides. A hosted blog will most likely offer one format or the other (Blogger offers Atom and WordPress offers RSS). On our blogs, we offer both formats because it's easy to do and doesn't require any more work. It also gives our readers a choice. If they want an Atom feed instead of an RSS one, they can have it.

Feed Broadcast Options

If you use a newsreader, you'll notice that the blogs you're subscribed to show up in the reader in different ways. When you set up your blog, you will have to choose from one of three broadcast options.

- Broadcast the headline only: In this case, people will see only the headline in their newsreaders and must click through to your Web site to read any of the blog post. This appeals to some bloggers because they feel it strongly motivates people to come to their site. We're not so sure about this. More and more people we talk to feel headline-only feeds are frustrating because they require extra steps to actually read the content and are dropping their subscriptions to sites that only offer this limited option.

- Broadcast the headline and partial copy: Partial copy displays the first few sentences of your posts. You'll get more subscribers to your feeds than the previous option, and people will click through to your main site if they want the full story.

- Broadcast the headline and full copy: People generally like being able to stay in their newsreader and read everything there, so your feeds will be embraced fully, and you'll get the most readers of your content. The problem is that if you have ads or other promotional material on your Web site that you'd like readers to see, this brings your site the fewest visitors.

Most of the business bloggers we've talked to are primarily interested in getting more visitors to come to their Web site. If that's the case for you, we advise partial-copy broadcasts. Headlines-only will result in dropped subscriptions, and full-copy feeds result in far fewer click-throughs.

 TIP: Be aware that if you're publishing partial-copy RSS feeds, the first line of the post has to be compelling and to the point. Otherwise readers will be bewildered, won't know what the post is about, and won't click through. We'll cover how to write for blogs in Chapter 6, "Writing Your Blog," and offer tips on how to engage your readers.

On some of our sites, we offer both partial- and full-feed links and let the readers decide which they prefer. This is a good option for blogs where you are interested in maximizing readership, and click-through is nice but not critical.

Email Notification

In addition to RSS, you can offer your readers a way to be notified by email when you post. Notifications work just like electronic newsletter subscriptions and are easy to set up. There are a variety of online services, such as FeedBlitz, that help bloggers integrate these email notifications into their blogs. While more knowledgeable surfers will prefer to receive your content via RSS, notifications are great for a less technical audience that hasn't fully embraced RSS yet.

Other Features to Consider

Once you've got the basics down, it's time to consider all the other features that'll make your site brim with bloggy goodness. Features like comments and trackbacks offer lots of benefits, but also require more work, time, and resources.

Comments

Almost all blog engines and services provide the capability for readers to attach their thoughts, insights, and/or arguments directly to the posts they're reading. These comments (and responses to comments) can provide for a rich dialog between bloggers and readers that can drive attention and traffic. Comments can also be used as an indicator of reader interest. The more comments a post receives, the more likely it will be that people find it compelling.

While comments can provide tangible traffic and dialog benefits, they require some effort to do right. As we described in Chapter 3, "How Much Blog — and How Often?" you'll want to be sure to have the hours available to monitor, approve, and respond to the comments that come in. GM's Fastlane blog (*http://fastlane.gmblogs.com/*) has staff that just manages comments, while Boeing runs their comments like an old-fashioned editorial page, vetting the comments and selecting just a handful to post.

Balancing Risks and Benefits

As you set up your first blog, you'll need to decide how you'll want to manage the comments that come in. As most experienced bloggers have learned, an open "anything goes" policy has some significant drawbacks.

One of the main reasons you'll want to monitor and filter comments is to combat comment spam, which is becoming a significant problem for bloggers. Comment spammers use automated Web "robots" that can browse thousands of blogs in rapid succession looking for opportunities to insert random "comments" promoting their wonderful online casino offerings or various pharmaceutical products. One reason why comment spam exists is so that spammers can gain valuable inbound links. By inserting comments on your blog that contain links back to their sites, they hope to trick Google into thinking that their site is highly relevant because so many other sites link back to them.

Other challenges include dealing with obscenities, off-topic remarks, and the occasional troublemaker who has an ax to grind.

One option is to simply turn comments off and not allow them at all. For the blogger who is very tight on time and doesn't want the hassle, this can be a viable choice.

We normally suggest that businesses avoid this rather one-sided option and instead implement the Comment Moderation or Filtering feature. Common filtering options provided by many blog software systems include:

- Preauthorization of posts: This is an approach we employ on the Blog Business Summit site. When a reader comments to the system, the author of the original post is automatically sent an email containing the comment and a link to authorize, delete, or edit the comment being submitted. After a few comments from the same person have been approved, their comments are posted automatically. By allowing our regular readers to earn our trust, we give them a feeling of being a special member of our community. This also cuts down on the amount of approving we have to do.

- Anti-robot comment system: In many systems, the comment form contains a "test" that robots find hard to pass. Usually, a graphic with an embedded word is presented to the viewer who must correctly enter that word into a field for validation.

- Semi-automated exclusion tools: Some blog engines allow the owner to enter specific banned words and/or IP addresses of commenters to be excluded. When the system encounters the blacklisted words or banned individuals, their posts are ignored.

Of course, none of the automated approaches can completely replace hands-on monitoring and moderation. We'll discuss the art of comment and community management more fully in Chapter 8, "Monitoring and Managing Your Blog."

Trackbacks

The problem with standard comments is that when you write them, you're working hard to add valuable content to someone else's blog. Wouldn't you rather just be contributing to your own site? Wouldn't it be better if you could write a response or rebuttal post on your own site and then have it also magically appear as a comment on the blog you're referencing? That way you'd get double credit for your effort. This is what trackbacks allow you to do.

Here's how trackbacks work. Let's say you read a blog post that says, "The world is made out of snow," and you feel strongly that there is evidence that suggests otherwise. Rather than click the Comment link at the bottom of their post, look for a link that says "Trackback" and right-click it to copy that link location. Then head back to your own blog and make a post with your rebuttal. Inside the form where you enter your post, look for a box that says "Ping" or "Trackback" and then paste in the link. Your blog will automatically notify the other site that the comment has been made, and the other site will likely display it.

Technically speaking, a trackback is a Web technology that lets a Web page know which other pages on the Web link to it; the blogs ping each other, which is a fancy way of saying "Hello. I'm here with new content."

The promise of trackbacks is significant. They make it very easy for bloggers to track how their posts are received by the blogosphere. But like other promising technologies, trackbacks are vulnerable to nefarious spammers, who can flood your site with bogus links. Because of this, we only turn trackbacks on during Blog Business Summit events, to capture the "live blog conversation." We don't use them at all on our other blogs. We recommend that if you do use trackbacks, watch them closely to prevent a flood of bad or spammy links.

Search

As your blog gets larger and contains more and more posts, category and keyword links alone may not provide your readers with everything they need to find specific information easily.

One of the best ways to make sure visitors have easy access to all posts on your site is to provide a search box in the sidebar. With a search option specific to your blog, readers can look for posts containing any keywords they choose.

Another great reason to add search to your site is to make it easy for you to find previous posts that you want to reference when writing new ones. Many times we've found ourselves wanting to update a story that we wrote long ago, and being able to quickly find the older reference made that task much easier.

Luckily, adding search to your blog site is quite easy. Most blog-hosting programs have built-in search capability, and usually provide preformatted page templates that include a search box positioned in the sidebar.

Many experienced bloggers choose not to use the built-in search function their software provides and instead will incorporate a blog-specific Google search box. Some claim that this "Google Free WebSearch" service returns results in a format they find more useful. It's also a great choice for TypePad users and other people with blog software that lacks built-in search capability. The Google Free WebSearch is simply a snippet of free HTML code available on Google's site that can be copied and pasted into your sidebar. Google requires that you register for a "Google Free" account—which, as the name suggests, costs nothing—in order to receive working code.

The only real disadvantages to using Google's search service is that advertisements will appear in the results pages, and your blog will need to be already indexed within Google's database for it to work. In other words, if a regular Google search for your site comes up empty, this service will not find any results either until your blog has been indexed. It won't take long at all for Google and other search engines to find your site after you start posting. We'll talk more about this in Chapter 7, "Launching Your Blog and Getting Noticed."

TIP: If you're publishing a blog from your own servers, make sure that you've told search engine robots that it's okay to index your site with a robots.txt file (you can also tell them not to index it, if you choose). For more about robots.txt, see *www.robotstxt.org*.

Calendars

Almost all blog engines allow a calendar to be displayed in the sidebar, as shown in **Figure 4.7**. Calendars show what days of any month have posts associated with them, and specific days can be clicked to see what has been posted on that date.

Calendars are not for everyone. They take up a lot of space and may also emphasize how infrequently you post. We believe that readers are less interested in what you said on November 23rd and are more likely looking to find posts by topic, title, tag, and category.

Figure 4.7

Mezzoblue is the blog (*www.mezzoblue.com*) of Web designer and author Dave Shea. Dave encourages readers to browse and explore his archives by offering multiple views organized by date, links to most recent posts, and a calendar view.

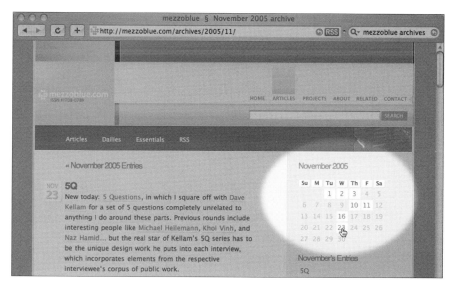

Design Considerations

One of the things that separates a good blog from a great one is how well designed it is.

Consider one of the biggest home run products of the decade, Apple's iPod. There were scores of other portable digital music players available years before Apple got into the game, yet none of them gained more than a tiny fraction of the attention and market share that the iPod did. The reasons for this success are fairly clear. The iPod is a device with great features, utilizing a highly approachable interface and presented in a form that is visually appealing.

Making a priority of integrating form and function together has proven to be a winning combination for Apple, and the same is true for many of the top blogs.

In this section, we'll discuss techniques top bloggers use to make sure that their sites are visually appealing, provide full access to the features visitors want, and deliver on critical business goals.

Page Layout

You've probably noticed that the vast majority of blogs have very similar layouts. There's usually a banner on top, navigation elements, and two or three columns of content.

Column layouts, like newspapers and magazines, are well suited to blogs because of the way posts are created in chronological order and stored by the database. English reading patterns from left to right and then down are conducive to the column format. Columns also permit white space and rules between them so your content is easy to read, not overly crowded or visually complex.

We suspect that you'll want to employ a column layout, but you are not locked into that form. If you hire a designer who understands blogs, he or she can create a custom template that has a more unique approach and can best express the personality of your business. For example, you may choose to blend bloglike features into your existing site, like post headlines and RSS. We'll talk more about unique uses for blogs in Chapter 9, "Beyond Blogging."

If your blog is of the variety offered by a hosted service, picking a layout couldn't be easier. You just choose the layout from a list of available templates, as shown in **Figure 4.8**, click Save, and you're done.

Figure 4.8

Blogger offers well-designed templates you can choose for your blog layout.

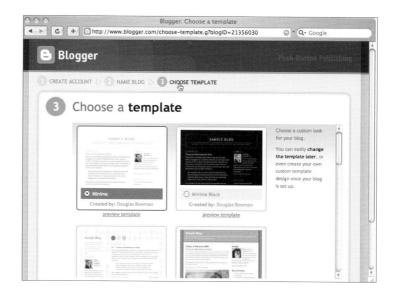

It's a safe bet that no matter what blog software engine you decide to use to host your blog, you will have a rich set of options for controlling the layout of your pages. Number and width of columns and location of elements within those columns will be under your complete control.

Deciding What Goes Where

Now that you have a better idea of what items you want to include in your blog, you need to consider where to put them and how to get them there.

It matters where you put things on your pages, just like it matters where stores put things on the shelves. In all modern supermarkets, the goods and the shelves they sit on are carefully positioned to make it easy for shoppers to find and buy the things they need (and often to buy things they don't need!).

For example, there's a good reason that high-profit items like meat and seafood are positioned along the entire back length of supermarkets. It's so you'll see them every time you're at the end of an aisle.

A similar situation exists on the Web. Amazon.com is constantly testing new layouts, offers, and product positioning to determine what variables induce people to click and buy. Online retailers spend millions of dollars every year trying to optimize their pages to yield more profitability. These sites clearly want surfers to stay as long as possible, and hope visitors navigate to specific pages they target as important.

Even though you may not be offering products directly for sale on your blog, no doubt you have specific goals in mind for the people who visit. Maybe you want visitors to fill out a survey form or read about the services you offer. Perhaps you're hosting ads on your site and would like surfers to click on them. Whatever your ultimate goals are, where you put things makes a big difference.

Even though you may not have big bucks to spend on visitor usability research, there is a lot of valuable information freely available that can help you determine where the priority items should go.

It's widely accepted that the most important content (the things you really want people to notice) should be positioned on the first screen visible to visitors when they land on your site. The items that sit "above the fold" will get more attention than content that requires scrolling to read or see. Eye-tracking research has proven this, and has provided us with other useful conclusions.

WHAT IS "ABOVE THE FOLD"?

The term "above the fold" is borrowed from newspaper editors. It is where the important news story or photograph should be located on the front of the paper in the top half, above where the paper is folded. In traditional Web site design, "above the fold" describes what could be viewed in a browser without scrolling.

Eye-tracking systems use cameras and infrared beams to determine where people look when sitting in front of a computer. Several researchers have used this technology to determine what parts of Web pages and blogs are of most interest to readers. In other words, science tells us what parts of Web pages typically get the most (and least) attention. Based on their research, Eyetools, Inc. has created a diagram that shows general viewer "priority zones" for a single screenful of Web page information. The darkest boxes shown in **Figure 4.9** are the areas that receive the most attention.

Figure 4.9

Eye-tracking research done by Eyetools, Inc. and the Poynter Institute has defined the relative zones of onscreen attention. The darkest areas indicate where people look the most on Web pages.

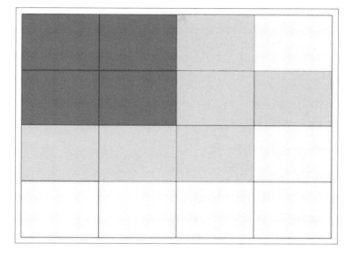

Clearly, the upper-left part of the page is where you should put items you want people to notice most, and the lower-right part is where the least critical information should go. Items that fall below this full-screen area and require scrolling are those that are the least important.

For example, if the main goal of your blog is to increase sales of a specific product, you'd want to put information about that product in the upper-left corner with a link to buy.

While given enough effort and custom code, you can pretty much put anything anywhere on a page; 99.9 percent of blogs have a banner area at the top of every page identifying and describing the site.

Repositioning or eliminating that banner is usually not something people want to do, and hosted blog software programs don't make it easy to move or get rid of it. For these reasons, we will assume that any blog you'll do will have an identifying banner at the top of every page.

HOW MANY COLUMNS?

Blog-hosting services universally offer predesigned templates with layouts that can present your content in one-, two-, or three-column designs. Many designers feel that the one- or two-column layout is the cleanest, and best emphasizes the posts you write. One key problem with one- and two-column layouts is that they don't provide as much usable real estate on your pages as three-column layouts do, and more sidebar items need to be put below the fold, forcing people to scroll down in order to see them. That's the main reason professional blogs (versus personal diary blogs) seem to lean toward a three-column layout.

There are those who say that three columns lead to more cluttered layouts that can confuse users. We tend to disagree with that sentiment. We have seen many clean, attractive, and functional three-column layouts over the years. In addition, Amazon.com has tested the effectiveness of their layouts for years, and the evidence is overwhelming that in practically all of their tests, "clean" one- and two-column layouts don't sell nearly as well as three-column ones containing lots of options above the fold.

How Do You Change the Layout?

Rearranging elements and columns is fairly straightforward and easy with hosted systems like TypePad and Blogger. All you need to do is log into the system and click on the options they make available.

To change the layout of a customized blog hosted by programs like Movable Type or WordPress, which run on a server that you manage, you'll need to have a team member with basic Web designer/developer skills and administrator access to the Web server. These systems usually require your designer to edit the code for the template layout you are using, and then upload that modified template to the server.

How Much Time Will It Take?

On a hosted application, you should be up and running with an impressive layout in about five or ten minutes max. For customized self-hosted blogs with lots of features, it will take about a day to get running. The day is spent installing, configuring, and creating the layout templates.

Remember that once you set up the system, you won't have to touch the configuration again until you decide to change the features or design.

Fonts

When designing for readers, one of the most important decisions you will make is which typefaces to use for your blog. While you have a vast array of fonts to choose from when you design the site, only a small number of fonts are appropriate for use in most blogs.

Except in a few special cases, Web pages can only be displayed using the fonts already present on any given user's computer. If possible, you'll want to choose a font that the reader has installed on their system. If you choose a font that the reader does not have available, their browser software will automatically choose a substitute. That replacement font could be something inconsistent with your design or might be significantly less readable than what you intended. Most blog templates specify fonts that are widely installed, but it's something to be aware of if you choose to customize your template or design your own.

On our blogs, we frequently use the Verdana typeface, which was designed to be displayed and read on a computer screen. Verdana is widely available and is preinstalled on most computers, across many different platforms including Macintosh, Windows, and Unix. Other commonly installed screen-friendly fonts include Georgia and Trebuchet.

Bigger Is Better

A computer screen is like a tiled wall. Coloring individual "tiles" (or pixels) on the screen makes images appear. The trend has been for screens to get larger and the pixels to get smaller. The result is that every year Web designers have larger "walls" to work with, and with ever-smaller "tiles."

One of the resulting trends is for designers of Web pages and blogs to specify large font sizes—sometimes really large: 14 pixels tall for sentences and all the way up to 60 pixels for headings.

We agree that larger fonts are good, because they make content easy to read, but you don't want to overdo it and end up yelling each headline and paragraph at your readers.

USING FLASH TO DELIVER RICH TYPOGRAPHY

There is a very handy utility that allows Web designers and savvy bloggers to design their pages to include any typeface they desire. This approach displays fonts that look great—even on the screens of visitors that don't have that specific font installed. Perhaps you have a corporate typeface that you really want to use, or have another specific font that you feel is ideal for your blog. Flash technology allows you to use any font you want.

Flash is a Web media format that was originally developed to deliver animation and high-quality illustrations over the Internet. Many popular online greeting cards, games, and cartoons are delivered using Flash, and it's become one of the most widely used Web graphic formats.

Flash requires that Web surfers have the Flash player software installed as a plug-in within their Web browser, and more than 97 percent of Web surfers are currently in that position. Even if a visitor does not have Flash, all that means is that a font you specify (like Verdana) will be substituted.

Colors

With a hosted application like Blogger or TypePad, you can pick the colors for your blog from a selection of professionally designed templates. Talented designers have laid out these preformatted pages, and they've done a great job of selecting colors that are pleasing and professional. If you're hosting your own blog and are using a program like Movable Type or WordPress, you'll likely hire your own designer to lay out and choose the right colors for your blog.

If you're customizing your blog and want to create your own template, you might want to start with the colors used in your company's marketing materials. Chances are you already have a logo with matching colors and can just reuse those. Many companies just add a blog to their existing site structure and match the appearance of the already established pages.

One method that we often use is to pick natural colors from a digital photograph, like a brick building or landscape. We open the photo in a photo-editing application, use the Eyedropper tool to select the most prominent colors, and then use them as swatches for our blog designs. For the color-challenged, try *www.colorcombos.com*. You start with a color you like, and the site will create matching swatches for you to use. The design site Colors on the Web (*www. webwhirlers.com/colors/colorwizard.asp*) contains a number of useful articles, tools, and tips to assist you in choosing colors that work well together.

Remember that blogs are meant to be more casual and relaxed, and you should use soft, earthy, warm colors like orange and green. Think J. Crew catalog instead of IBM blue (unless, of course, you're IBM).

Usability and Accessibility

The ultimate Web site is simple for people to navigate, can be accessed easily by those with disabilities, and can be read on a variety of devices including cell phones and PDAs. In the early days of the Web, if you tried to build a Web site that achieved these goals using standard HTML, you discovered quickly that it was extremely difficult.

In 1998, a group of Web designers came together to make these (and many other) jobs easier for people who build Web sites. They created an organization called the Web Standards Project (WaSP). Their intent was to create a set of standards for building Web sites that would make it much simpler to design sites that worked correctly in a variety of environments.

Many Web developers and designers now adhere to "standards-based design" and build their pages using the guidelines and tools enabled by WaSP.

Many of these early WaSP adherents went on to design the blogging systems in use today, and the result is that the pages these systems create are almost always automatically highly compliant with standards-based design. One of the big benefits of this is that blog sites generally adhere to Section 508, the federal law that requires government agencies to ensure that Web sites are accessible to individuals with disabilities. The clean, structured content of blogs is ideally suited for the audio screen readers used by the blind.

The standards-based architecture of blog sites means that devices like cell phones and PDAs can easily display your posts and other blog content. Most HTML pages look like a garbled mess on these tiny screens, so blogging opens up a vast audience that many traditional Web sites can't reach. We've seen this firsthand. One of Clip-n-Seal's earliest sales was to a customer who commuted to work on a ferry. The customer was able to browse, view, and purchase the product with his PDA because our site was blog-based. This easy accessibility also applies to non-PC equipment like PlayStations, Xboxes, or pretty much any other Web-surfing devices.

HIRING A DESIGNER

While a blog should offer bloggy features, it doesn't necessarily have to look like all the other blogs based on templates that the hosted services provide. If you don't have a designer on staff, we suggest you hire one. The cost shouldn't be that high, because the designer generally only has to design two or three template pages that your blog engine will use to build every page on the site. If you want to build a larger blog for a community, or a network of blogs, consider hiring developers and designers. In this case, your budget is going to be considerably larger, in the range of a traditional Web site.

Iterative Design

As a final note, remember that a blog is meant to be flexible. You don't have to go through a rigid design and development process to launch the blog or change the style. Feel free to try different layouts, move the content around, and update the features. You can make most of the changes on the fly, with your blog engine.

Now that you have a better understanding of what elements and design choices can make for a superior blog, you'll want to wrap those components into the right blogging engine.

Selecting the right software platform for hosting your blog will ensure that you minimize expense and effort while maximizing flexibility and power.

In the next chapter, we'll take a closer look at the various blog-hosting options you have to choose from, and discuss what factors you should consider before taking the plunge.

Chapter 5

Tools and Implementation

There are a vast number of technologies and tools available to help make your blog a success. The problem is that you can't use them all, and once you've made your choices, replacing one technology with something more appropriate to your needs can raise thorny migration issues. In this chapter, we'll discuss some of the essential blog-related software and services that you have to choose from, and what you should factor into your decision making. Later in the chapter, we also offer a handy chart that lays out your options for you.

Once you decide on the software you'll be using, there are further technology-related decisions to make. How do you prefer to post? Will you be offering audio or video podcasts? Will you have advertising on your blog? Do you need to manage the authoring process and want to add lots of cool features? We'll walk you through the major decisions that lie ahead and offer guidance to make sure you hit the ground running with your blog and start publishing and prospering.

Assessing Your Blogs

The tools and services that bloggers have at their disposal vary widely in terms of price, functionality, and technical requirements. A thorough assessment of your organization and the players involved can quickly cut through much of the confusion.

Picking the right tools and technologies is important for any effort you make. It's safe to say that you won't need a parachute on a cruise ship, or bug repellent on a trip to Antarctica. On the other hand, you had better take a Sherpa guide with you if you're going climbing in the Himalayas. Knowing exactly what kind of "trip" you're going to take into the blogosphere (and who will join you) can ensure that you don't pack the wrong equipment.

How Many Blogs?

Consider whether you may want to end up hosting multiple blogs. Many companies that have dipped their toes into the world of blogging have ultimately decided that they want several or even all of their employees to have blogs. Some hosting platforms accommodate this type of growth, and others do not. It is a good idea to ponder this question early in order to determine which engine will serve you for both the short and long term.

How Many Bloggers?

Even if you host only one blog, you may decide that you want multiple authors or writers posting to that blog. It is critical to research how the various services and software packages support this.

Can you allow multiple authors at all? Can those authors be given different levels of permission? For example, you may decide that you'd like to review the posts of some authors before they are put up on the site. You may want to empower others to directly post to the site without review.

Another workflow issue related to having multiple authors is the ability to post remotely. Some blog services and engines allow for submitting posts via email, and others do not.

What Kind of Technical Resources Are Available to You?

Do you have access to staff or contractors who are proficient in doing geeky things like configuring Web servers, building HTML pages, or installing databases? If so, this puts you in an entirely different camp than a small business operator who must perform all Web site administration. Having access to technical staff broadens your options and your flexibility in how you host your blog, and what kind of capabilities you can include.

How Much Control Do You Need?

Do you generally want to have as much control as you can over your technology-related ventures, or are you more concerned with getting the main benefits with as little effort as possible? With blogging, you have many options on the continuum between easy (with limited control) and full control (with more effort required).

When you have performed at least a cursory assessment of your business needs, you'll be better prepared for the next section, where we dive into some of the specifics of the various blogging engines and services.

Selecting a Software System or Service

While blogging tools are remarkably consistent in their core attributes and features (database architecture, permalinks, syndicated feeds, layout and design flexibility, etc.), there are still big differences between them. Picking an unsuitable platform and then having to change later to the "right" tool can be time-consuming and could even result in a big drop in readership.

In this section, we'll cover the types of popular blog tools and what advantages and disadvantages exist for each. The table at the end of this section puts it all together.

Hosted Systems

If you want to get blogging quickly, easily, and without a lot of technical hassles, a hosted service may be the way for you to go. Services like TypePad, Blogger, WordPress.com, LiveJournal, and MSN Spaces provide the software and predesigned page templates for you. All you have to do is sign up for an account online, choose a blog layout and style, and within minutes you can start posting.

If you've ever had an email account that you accessed via a Web browser such as Hotmail, you have a feel for what using a dedicated hosted service is like. As with Hotmail and other Web-based email services, you are provided with an account and you interact with the service via an online connection using your browser.

These services are not expensive. Many are free, and even the priciest ones we've seen cost less than $20 a month.

With a hosted service, you can configure your blog, write posts, and adjust layouts using a Web browser from any computer with an Internet connection. You can post, change designs, and control what elements are on your pages from just about anywhere.

In general, you cannot access any of the programs or scripts on the server, nor can you modify any server configuration or database settings.

Several of these hosted blog solutions have worked hard to create blogging systems with high-end features, and many of the top business bloggers use this style of blog to successfully manage their publishing and online conversations.

Advantages

There is no easier or less expensive way to blog than with a hosted service. You don't have to install or maintain software, manage a server, or deal with supporting users. This leaves you free to focus on writing great posts.

The hosted services have generally put a lot of time, effort, and money into creating a large variety of attractive templates and have provided simple ways to customize your pages so that you can create an attractive site without having to hire a designer.

Hosted services will often make other bloggers who use the same service aware of your site. For example, TypePad presents a set of "recently updated" sites on their main login page. This is a nice little bit of extra publicity for your blog.

Disadvantages

One of the main reasons that many blogging pros decide not to go with a hosted service has to do with how domain names are managed. By design, hosted services will present your blog as being hosted from a subdomain under their name. Instead of your posts being seen at *www.acmewidgets.com*, they're appearing at *acmewidgets.typepad.com* or *acmewidgets.blogspot.com*.

Many companies feel that this projects an unprofessional image, and if you have a site already up at *www.acmewidgets.com*, it means that visitors and search engines aren't paying as much attention to your "main" site.

Having your posts held under someone else's domain also makes it much more difficult to switch to a different service and to migrate your old posts to the new location. This wreaks havoc with search engines and bookmarks.

You can partially get around this limitation by using techniques like domain name forwarding, and/or domain name mapping. By redirecting URLs and using other geeky techniques, it's possible to have posts held by some hosted systems appear to be located under a different domain, but it's not a perfect solution. If you're committed to using a hosted system, you'll want to talk with your technical staff (or a consultant) to determine if this is a reasonable option.

The inability to manage what happens on the server can also be quite limiting, especially for those who are used to expanding a site's functionality via scripting or custom programming. A time may come when an important option you'd like to include on your site may be impossible to add because it requires a server modification.

For example, an experienced blogger we know recently told us about a company that pays to put ads on blogs, and they compensate him significantly better than any of the other advertisers he's worked with. This ad broker requires bloggers to install a small script on their servers to automate their ad placements, so those using a hosted service can't take advantage of these lucrative ads.

Another reason many companies reject the idea of using a hosted service is that they plan to have many employees blogging. Setting up an individual account for each blog and blogger can be time-consuming and potentially quite expensive for large companies. That kind of fragmentation can also make managing these blogs and bloggers difficult.

You should also consider things like downtime and maintenance. There will be times when your hosted service will go down and your site will be unavailable. Two of the largest services, Blogger and TypePad, have seen outages that have lasted several hours at a time. And if you are not hosting the blog yourself, you will have little to no control over how or when it will come back up. If a blog on your own servers goes down, you have access to the people who are directly in charge of getting things back up and running.

Another critical aspect that all businesses should consider is that the major hosting services have the option to shut down your site, anytime, and at their discretion. We've reviewed the terms of service for TypePad, Blogger, Live Journal, and MSN Spaces and have discovered that they generally reserve the right to terminate your account for any reason. A few other services, such as WordPress.com, don't provide any terms of service whatsoever.

Many businesses have determined that this raises an unacceptable level of risk. Whatever you decide, you'll want to consider these factors, in addition to potential long-term issues like the future financial health of the hosting company.

Installed Systems

In contrast to hosted services, where a complete blog tool is already set up and you simply become a subscriber, installed systems offer businesses the capability to set up and manage their own blog publishing systems.

If you or members of your team are comfortable with dealing with a Web server, then installing your own blog software may be the way for you to go. There are a wide variety of software programs available for purchase (as well as for free) that you can download and install on your own Web servers.

The higher-end systems that meet most business needs include programs such as WordPress (which offers both hosted and installed systems), Movable Type, Drupal, and many others.

You don't actually need to have a physical server of your own set up to use these programs. Server-based blog publishing tools can be installed either on your own server or on a computer located with an Internet service provider (ISP). Verio, Interland, and most of the other popular hosting companies will let you install and manage blog programs on their machines remotely.

Installing and running blog software on your (or an ISP's) Web server will give you a great deal of control over almost every aspect of your blog. Even if your blog software lacks capabilities, it's often possible to install scripts or plug-ins that will modify how the software works.

Advantages

The main advantage of installing and managing your own server-based blog software is the degree of control and customization you have over your blog's features, configuration, and design. Custom page designs, optional features, additional storage space, and the benefits from custom programming are all available to you. You can generally add more users and blogs at will, and can control what levels of access they have to the various sites being published.

You also completely eliminate the problems associated with having a hosting service's domain name visible. You get to use your own domain name, so visitors will never see a URL that references another organization.

Related to this domain name advantage is that of long-term flexibility. Since the blogs are under your domain, the pathnames can stay the same if you decide to switch to a different blog program. This means permalinks will stay intact. In layman's terms, this means you can take your entire blog down and reconstitute it using different software and Google won't know the difference. All your old posts will remain easily findable.

It also means that if your ISP goes out of business and shuts down your blog, you can relaunch it at a new ISP, and all of your posts will stay right where the search engines think they belong.

This stands in stark contrast to what happens when a hosted service shuts down or if you decide to switch to another blog platform. In that case, the pathnames and permalinks are generally much more difficult (or even impossible!) to recreate. Broken and/or bad links can greatly reduce your visibility and relevance in the blogosphere.

Disadvantages

Server-based blog software requires installation, configuration, administration, customization, and support. You will need to assemble a team that can deal with these tasks. As we said in Chapter 4, "Designing for Readers," budget a full day of effort to get a basic system up and running, and then a couple hours a week of administrative effort to perform maintenance, backups, and maybe a few scripting and database-related tasks.

Compared to hosted services, many of these installed blog programs do not provide as many predesigned page templates or have the degree of integrated features that allow you to easily modify colors, fonts, or layouts. This means you'll likely want to get a professional designer on board to create template pages, and will occasionally want to bring them in to make modifications. This will impose some expenses and delays that can be avoided with the hosted blogging services.

While the cost of the software itself is generally minimal ($20 to $40 per user), you should factor in the labor costs related to installation, management, design, and administration. For most small and mid-sized businesses, more cash will be spent running your blogs on installed systems than would be spent using a hosted service.

HYBRID HOSTING SERVICES: THE BEST OF BOTH WORLDS?

A new type of blogging engine alternative has begun to emerge. Companies like Yahoo! Small Business are offering to manage installed systems for you, while charging a monthly fee. You sign up for an account, just like with a hosted service, but you'll also get access to a Movable Type or WordPress installation (normally something you'd have to install on your own servers).

With this scenario, you get much of the best of both worlds. They manage the servers, install the software, and you can just log in and access a more powerful blog solution. They even install some of the most popular scripts and plug-ins, so you get even more features. Using your own domain name is possible as well.

Custom-Built Systems

If you have smart programmers at your disposal (or if you know how to code for the Web), the ultimate in control and customization can be yours if you create your own blogging system from scratch.

Many software engineers who have "rolled-their-own" blog software prefer this approach because it provides the greatest flexibility, and the software can be designed to more closely match how the people involved want to work.

Interested developers will discover that there are many prewritten blog software components available for popular development languages like PHP and ASP.NET, and these modules can be readily assembled to create custom blog engines.

In addition, there are several new programming environments, such as Ruby on Rails, which are particularly well-suited to creating blogging applications, and advocates claim that a highly functional system can be built very quickly using these environments.

Despite these advantages, there is less reason these days to start from scratch and build your own blog engine. This is partly because the prewritten engines have matured significantly over time. Thanks to many years of development, the most vexing limitations of the early blogging applications have been largely overcome.

The existing engines also tend to be extensible, which means that you can buy or program plug-ins to add features as needed without having to completely reinvent the wheel.

Another great reason to use an existing engine is that you can tap into an established user community for support and guidance. There are many forums, blogs, articles, and other resources available that can answer questions, refer consultants, or guide you to software add-ons or enhancements.

One thing is certain: You want to avoid the temptation to make your own diary-style site by hand-building HTML pages that appear to look "bloggy." More than a few people we know have tried to begin "blogging" this way, and all have eventually regretted it. The lack of RSS feeds, permalinks, comments, and the inconvenience of hand-coding make this a dismal alternative. You also stand a good chance of being criticized by the blogosphere for having a "pseudo-blog."

Enterprise-Level Systems

For some organizations, only a large-scale, industrial-strength blogging solution will provide the functionality they're looking for. Publicly held companies that have strict regulatory requirements, or those that want to empower many employee bloggers will want to take a serious look at the high-end "enterprise" blogging applications.

Programs like those provided by Marqui, iUpload, Traction Software, Six Apart, blogtronix, and others go far beyond being just enhanced versions of server-installed blog engines. Enterprise blog software focuses on providing features that carefully control and track how content is published.

While blogging can do wonderful things for a business, there are significant risks—especially for those organizations that fall under the requirements of Sarbanes-Oxley or Regulation FD (Fair Disclosure). Regulation FD makes revealing "material nonpublic information" illegal. A blogger who inadvertently posts too early about the "great quarter" they've had could see expensive civil penalties being levied against him and/or the company.

Enterprise blog applications contain workflow features that provide for approval cycles. With regular blogging programs, entries are simply written and then go "live" with a click of a button. With Enterprise programs, posts can be screened, edited, and fact-checked prior to being published.

Approval and review is not just for employees that are posting. These systems can also filter out comments and trackbacks that might be damaging to your company's brand. Although conversation can be a great thing, visitors to your blog may provide negative feedback or language that you want to avoid on your site. Enterprise applications can help prevent angry rants or off-color commentary from going live.

These high-end blog engines have many other capabilities, including ones that appeal to those who need to keep accurate records. Most programs have the ability to track and recall all posts that are created, removed, and edited by specific individuals, and detailed activity and time reports can be generated.

There are usually intranet and project management features as well. Internal collaborative and communication tools are often a part of Enterprise blogging programs.

While these programs offer a great deal of power, they come at a cost. One can easily spend $5,000 to $10,000 and beyond to get a basic Enterprise system like this up and running. If you plan on having hundreds of users though, you may find the cost per user to be competitive with installed systems.

To assist you in choosing a blog platform, **Table 5.1** can give you some guidelines for what engine may be best for you.

Table 5.1

Blog Engine Summary

Category	Priority	Resources	Engine
Small/home office business (solo consultant, author, etc.)	Ease of setup and administration	Largely self-reliant	Hosted service: TypePad, Blogharbor, Squarespace, etc.
Small business (1 to 10 bloggers)	Ease of setup and administration	Some technical consultants available, but avoid expense and complexity	Hosted service: TypePad, Blogharbor, Squarespace, etc.
Small business (1 to 10 bloggers)	Control: Flexibility to add features and desire maximum power from blogging system	Have technical and design staff or consultants readily available, and have budget available	Installed system: Movable Type, WordPress, TextPattern, Expression Engine, etc.
Corporate entity (1 to 50 bloggers)	Getting the dialog going; open culture, trusts employees to engage the blogosphere appropriately	Have in-house Web hosting and design expertise	Installed system: Movable Type, WordPress, TextPattern, Expression Engine, etc.
Enterprise, publicly held entity (potentially thousands of bloggers)	Stay in compliance with tight regulatory restrictions; manage large numbers of bloggers, and maintain tight control over what messages are communicated	Have a large IT department that manages a comprehensive array of Web and network services	Enterprise system: Marqui, Movable Type Enterprise, iUpload, WhatCounts, Traction Software, Blogtronix, etc.

NOTE: While throughout this book and in this table we mention some of the most prominent blogging engines, new engines are constantly being developed. These guidelines are not intended to act as endorsements for particular software. We suggest you follow these guidelines to do your own research to find the system that works for you.

Publishing Your Blog

Once you have your blog up and running, there are a variety of optional settings, tools, and technologies that can enhance your software and make your life a lot easier. In this section, we'll cover a few of the items that are very easy to set up yet can reap big dividends in terms of saving you time and expanding your reach.

Pinging and Publicity

Ping services are designed to let you notify the world that your site has been updated. If you tell your blog to inform these services whenever you post, it will almost certainly increase the number of people reading what you write.

There are millions of people who are using RSS search engines to find the latest information on topics of interest. Search engines like Technorati, PubSub, and Feedster monitor blog posts (and other RSS-related content) as new information is created. These engines not only let you search for specific terms, they also let you save those searches and will create a custom feed for you that can be brought into your newsreader software. The bottom line with RSS is that people can potentially subscribe to your blog's feed after discovering your blog, thanks to searches saved as feeds.

Imagine you run a Napa Valley winery and you write a post that mentions the release of your latest vintage Cabernet. If you have set your blog to ping, people who have saved Technorati searches with the words *Napa* and *Cabernet* will be notified very quickly. Depending on how you have set your feeds, they will receive your post headline and at least part of the post copy in their newsreader automatically.

This is one of the main ways that your blog will be discovered, and it's a primary reason that blogging has become so important to marketers. This can't happen in a timely fashion if you don't have pinging turned on. Pinging means that you don't have to wait for a blog search engine to drop by and notice what's new. Your ping tells it to drop by now, and update its records.

The two most widely used pinging services are Weblogs.com and Blo.gs (*http://blo.gs/*). Most blogging programs and services let you set these services to be notified when you update your site. Conversely, if you're setting up your blog in stealth mode and aren't yet ready to announce it, be sure to turn pinging off!

Posting from Your Desktop

You wouldn't do your word processing in a Web browser, would you? Even though there are several free Web sites that let you perform word processing and spreadsheet tasks, they're not very popular. The delays and start-and-stop nature of Web page loading (often referred to as latency issues) can make browser-based work quite frustrating.

This is the main reason that many experienced bloggers prefer to use desktop blog editors to create and edit their posts. Just like Microsoft Word, these editing applications run from your local hard drive and offer many advantages over the tired "click-and-wait" scenario.

Programs like Qumana, Blogjet, Ecto, and Blogger can be installed on your desktop computer and you can run them anytime—even when you're not connected to the Internet. You just launch the program, create a new post, and the only time you need to connect to the Web is when the post is submitted to the blog engine. There's no waiting for pages to load, no lost posts due to crashes, and editing is easier thanks to built-in features such as spell checking. Of course, you can also use Word, any text editor, or an HTML editor like BBEdit or Dreamweaver to write the posts and then enter them into your blog engine.

Podcasting and Media

Text posts are a great way to communicate with your market, but there are many other content options available to bloggers. Audio, video, and photographs are other types of media that your market might also find compelling. Thanks to the latest technologies for creating, editing, and distributing audio-visual media, it's now possible to find a large audience for "podcasts."

WHAT'S A PODCAST?

Podcasting is simply audio/video content that is alerted by an RSS feed. The term combines the words *broadcasting* and *iPod*. Despite the name's implications, the audio content is not actually broadcasted—users download it on demand—and you don't have to have an iPod to listen to it. Podcasting has become popular, just like blogging, because it can reach large audiences with relatively little effort on the part of the creator.

Back in the day, a storeowner built connections with customers by getting to know them in person, face-to-face, as a member of the community. Now businesses can have customers around the globe and never meet them. A blog is like a corner store in a global village, and you can give a friendly voice and a face to the storeowner with a video camera and a podcast. Podcasting is a very inexpensive way to build customer loyalty.

Podcasting transformed from an obscure techie diversion into a mainstream media outlet in less than a year. Podcasts are offered by all major media outlets, and there are over 30,000 podcasts available in iTunes, Apple's incredibly popular music store. It's been said that if there's a topic you're interested in, chances are there's a blog about it, and that's true of podcasts as well.

Millions of people worldwide are using portable media players (like the ubiquitous iPod) as tools for learning and keeping up with current events. These people are looking for quality content to listen to as they drive, work out, or do the dishes. As podcasting entrepreneur Eric Rice (*www.ericrice.com*) told us, "podcasting is a perfect way to offer customers relevant content that is less intrusive and more respectful of their time."

Many bloggers are now offering free audio podcasts. The word has spread that podcasts are a simple, easy way to deliver quality content, and that they're good for business. When we added weekly audio podcasts to our blogs, we saw traffic increase 50 percent, and other bloggers are claiming similar figures.

Tom Raftery is a blogger who runs an I.T. consultancy business in Ireland. His blog (*www.tomrafteryit.net)* covers topics related to Web technologies. Raftery says, "There was a marked increase in the number of visitors to my site after I added the podcast."

The number of visitors doubled in three months. As he says, "the bandwidth demands forced me to spin the podcast out into its own site (*podleaders.com*)."

Audio podcasts are simply digital sound recordings saved in the MP3 format that you create yourself and upload to your Web server. These sound files are then linked to an RSS feed, which makes them readily available to people using Apple's iTunes software or an RSS newsreader.

It's easy to create a podcast, and a quick Google search will find many pages with detailed instructions, but here are the basics: The first step is to digitally record some audio. If you connect a good microphone to your computer (built-in microphones are passable, but not ideal for voice recordings) and download some audio software, you're set. Many podcasters like the program Audacity, which is a free application for recording and editing sounds. Mac users can take advantage of Apple's powerful GarageBand application (**Figure 5.1**), which is an ideal tool for producing podcasts. After you've recorded the audio, you can use your editing software to remove pauses, coughs, and other unwanted bits. Finally, save the file to the MP3 format and upload it to your Web server.

Figure 5.1

Apple intends for GarageBand to be the preeminent application for managing podcast media and preparing audio for the Web.

PETS PODCASTING

For our first foray into podcasting, we created a podcast on Pugblog (*www.pugblog.com*), called a "pugcast." These humorous podcasts of Cap'n the pug barking caught on, got blogged, eventually made it into the iTunes podcast directory, and now drive considerable traffic. Purina foods recently launched a community site for pet owners with podcasts that offer advice, and there's even a serialized podcast novel (*www.huntingelf.com*), told from a dog's point of view.

Turning Audio Files into Syndicated Podcasts

By this point, you should be pretty comfortable with the idea that the text you enter into your blog posts can reach a wide audience thanks to RSS syndication. It's possible to syndicate audio files as well. Almost all hosted blog services and installed blog engine programs have features that will let you easily set media files (like MP3s) as RSS feed attachments.

Millions of people use RSS newsreaders such as NetNewsWire (**Figure 5.2**) and Juice to view content produced by bloggers, and that content can include audio files. These newsreaders will automatically download podcasts to your computer. All you do is subscribe to the RSS feeds, and your computer will handle the rest for you. Many of these programs integrate automatically with iTunes.

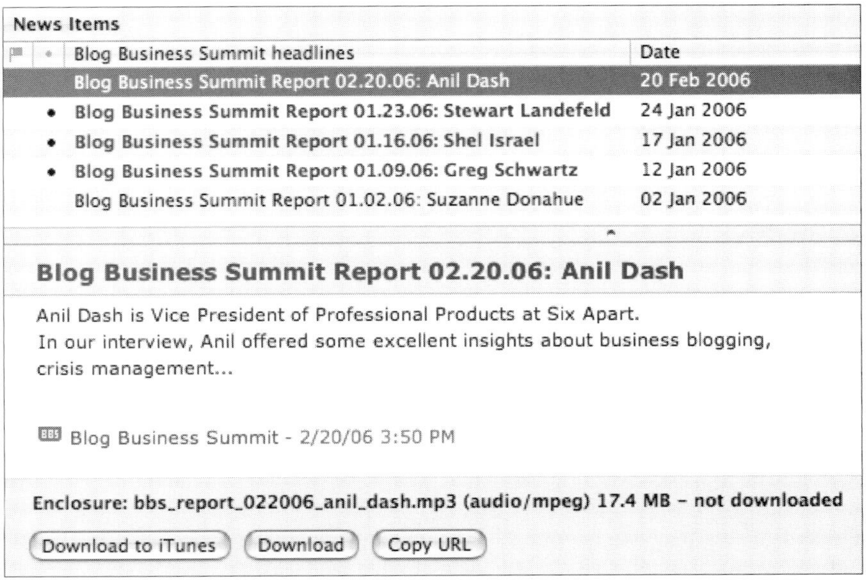

Figure 5.2

Posts that appear in most modern newsreaders can include more than text and images. Podcast links are now common.

News Items	
Blog Business Summit headlines	Date
Blog Business Summit Report 02.20.06: Anil Dash	20 Feb 2006
• Blog Business Summit Report 01.23.06: Stewart Landefeld	24 Jan 2006
• Blog Business Summit Report 01.16.06: Shel Israel	17 Jan 2006
• Blog Business Summit Report 01.09.06: Greg Schwartz	12 Jan 2006
Blog Business Summit Report 01.02.06: Suzanne Donahue	02 Jan 2006

Blog Business Summit Report 02.20.06: Anil Dash

Anil Dash is Vice President of Professional Products at Six Apart.
In our interview, Anil offered some excellent insights about business blogging, crisis management...

BBS Blog Business Summit - 2/20/06 3:50 PM

Enclosure: bbs_report_022006_anil_dash.mp3 (audio/mpeg) 17.4 MB – not downloaded

[Download to iTunes]   [Download]   [Copy URL]

After you have established an RSS feed link for your audio files, you can then submit that feed link to Apple's iTunes podcasting service. Having your podcast listed within Apple's directory can provide a significant amount of exposure, as millions of people search Apple's podcast database regularly for recordings that cover specific topics of interest. iTunes users can automatically receive your latest audio files as they are uploaded, and these recordings will even magically appear in their iPods when they synch to their computers.

Video Podcasts

An emerging media option for bloggers is that of posting video—also known as *vlogs*. Microsoft has been a pioneer in this arena with their Channel 9 offerings. Channel 9 is a popular vlog that receives tens of thousands of viewers daily. They present a behind-the-scenes view of Microsoft employees, designers, developers, and executives. Their videos consist largely of footage captured by roving cameramen that patrol the hallways of Microsoft.

We asked former Microsoft executive Lenn Pryor, who built Channel 9, about the launch of the service, and he said his goal was to "let the people behind the scenes be the stars." Consider what stars on your staff you could be video podcasting about!

MEDIA AND BANDWIDTH ISSUES

Audio files are big—and video files are even bigger, so be ready for a spike in bandwidth usage when you start podcasting in either medium. Your Web site hosts or Web team should offer tools to monitor and increase your bandwidth capacity when needed. You'll want to check with your hosted provider, like WordPress.com and TypePad, if appropriate, for any restrictions. You may need to upgrade to a higher service level to handle podcasting.

Photo Sharing

A photostream from the popular service at Flickr.com is a great way to present photos of yourself, friends, and coworkers on your blog. Businesses use the service to show the workplace, events, and products. Apple's iWeb service offers a photocasting feature, where readers can subscribe to your photo feed and get updates whenever you post new images.

While adding pictures, video, and audio is a simple process, there are a myriad of additional capabilities available to bloggers who are willing to roll up their sleeves and incorporate customized code into their pages, servers, and blog engines. In the next section, we'll look at how customizable blog software can be.

Enhancements and Add-ons

Take it from us, no matter how powerful your blog software is, or how basic you think your needs are, at some stage you'll invariably discover something "missing" from your blog software.

If there are useful features that you'd like to add to your blog engine, you're likely in luck. You can probably extend the power of your blogging software by using a variety of widely available programs and scripts or just writing your own.

Adding Features to Your Blog

At the most basic level, you can add various widgets to your pages by inserting either HTML or JavaScript code within your page templates. One example of this is covered in Chapter 4, when we added Google Search to a blog page. In that instance, it is simply a matter of copying and pasting a bit of code into the page. Most HTML or JavaScript page enhancements can be installed this way on blogs of all kinds, including hosted systems.

While adding small programmed goodies to pages is helpful, the most power comes from installing plug-ins within your blogging software or adding scripts to the server that hosts your pages. These techniques can add significant functionality to your blog. Installing plug-ins and server scripts are generally not possible with hosted services, but are fairly straightforward if you have a blog engine running on your own server or on an ISP's server.

The blogging community is generally ready, willing, and eager to share any scripted or programmed enhancements they develop. There are many sites such as *www.scriptygoddess.com* and *www.sixapart.com/pronet/plugins/* that feature scripts and plug-ins that are freely downloadable. This arena is quite mature now, and the odds are that if you have a feature you'd like to install, it's available.

Plug-ins and Scripts

Even after you've done intensive research and picked a blog engine that most closely matches your needs, you're likely to discover that there are additional features or capabilities that you wish you had available. Luckily, all of the common server-installed blogging software applications can be significantly enhanced by either adding scripts that modify how the server works, or by installing plug-ins that can modify how the blog application operates. Plug-ins and server scripts offer great power, but are generally not available to bloggers using a hosted service where users cannot access the server directly.

Most plug-ins are available as either shareware or freeware, and directories of what's available can be easily found via a Google search containing the name of your blog application and the word "plugin" or "plug-in." After you've found and downloaded a desired application, you'll need a technical guru to install, configure, and test it to make sure it's working properly.

Some of the more commonly requested features and capabilities that are available via plug-ins and scripts are described below.

Spam Filtering

Comment spam is what nefarious promoters do to enhance the visibility of their Web site within search engines. In a nutshell, they have robot computers troll the Internet looking for blogs containing posts they can "comment" on with the intent to insert a link back to their site. When they see a suitable post, a comment is inserted robotically. Comment spam often looks something like this: "I like your blog; keep up the good work! Play online poker here." Invariably, a link to the spammer's site is included, because the idea is to improve their Web site's page rank within Google by tricking the search engine into thinking people are linking to it. This type of spam can be embarrassing, as Blogger.com discovered when a spammer got past their filters and posted to their homepage (see **Figure 5.3**).

Figure 5.3

Ouch. These spammers will try to get their insidious comments and posts into just about any page that's popular, even the login page for Blogger.com.

Comment spammers often include multiple links in their comments, and some plug-ins can limit the number of links commenters are allowed to list. Other plug-ins can automatically eliminate comments that contain words or phrases common to spam (or contain words that you define).

On the Blog Business Summit site, we use a combination of a spam plug-in and moderation, which prevents a comment from going live until one of our contributors reviews and approves it.

Workflow

One of the greatest concerns businesses have regarding employee blogging is that management fears that they will "lose control" over what messages the company is sending out. Letting their employees simply broadcast their posts to the world without review can be a daunting proposition. With workflow plug-ins such as David Raynes' appropriately named Workflow and Moderate Authors plug-in for WordPress, posts can be passed by managers for approval before they are published live on the blog site.

Site Statistics

All blog services and server hosting companies provide rudimentary tools for tracking how many visitors your blog receives, but more in-depth reporting tools are available in both plug-in and script form. Shaun Inman's Mint and Google Analytics are both powerful script-based programs that can provide you with a particularly detailed look at what your visitors do when they come to your site.

WHAT ABOUT JAVASCRIPTS?

Savvy bloggers know that JavaScripts are simple bits of code that can be pasted directly into HTML Web page templates and can provide minor features and enhancements to those pages. Things like ads, survey forms, fields where visitors can ask to be notified via email of site updates, and blog search are common "widgets" that can be easily placed on your pages.

While JavaScripts are useful, don't confuse these with "server-side" scripts or blog software plug-ins that can precisely control how your blog database works. JavaScripts can't take control of the database that generates your blog pages; they can only play with how the pages look and act. If you want control over the data being held and manipulated by your blogging software, you'll need access to the server, and hosted services generally won't give you that access.

RSS and Syndication Enhancements

Most blogs blast out simple feeds to the world notifying readers of any (and all) new posts. This may not be what your readers are looking for. Sometimes you just don't want to order everything on the menu!

Depending on your blog software, many more selective and targeted syndication options may be available (especially for those using blogging engines installed on their own servers). Since "feed overload" is a complaint from many RSS subscribers, it's wise to provide your audience with the specific information they're looking for. Options can mean more people subscribing, and a higher level of interest from those who do receive your feeds.

The specifics of how (and if) your blog engine can support these enhanced syndication features will vary based on the software you use. Suffice it to say that plug-ins will likely exist for installed systems that can perform these functions, and hosted services won't have as many of these capabilities integrated.

Some of the targeted syndication options you should consider are discussed on the following pages.

Category Feeds

Even editorially focused blogs will likely contain posts that cover a wide variety of topics. Readers may want to hear about your new products, but won't necessarily want to know about upcoming trade shows you'll be attending. Since you'll be assigning categories to your posts, providing feeds that are category specific will allow visitors to subscribe to more focused areas of interest. Many installed systems will allow you to configure the system (or allow you to install plug-ins) to do this. Unfortunately, most hosted services do not have this feature built in (Squarespace is one of the few that does), but sometimes scripts or links from other filtering sites can enable category feeds.

Calendar Feeds

Subscribers will want to know what's on the organization's calendar. Colorado Ski Country has a blog whose readers are very interested in what festivities are coming up at their favorite resorts, so they offer a dedicated calendar feed for that purpose.

Author Feeds

Some blogs have multiple contributors, and readers may only want to subscribe to feeds from the specific authors that cover the subjects of most interest to them. For example, *The New York Times* offers RSS feeds that are specific to each writer.

Comment Feeds

More and more readers want to stay on top of not just blog posts, but also what comments are being made in response to those posts. The more powerful installed systems are now offering comment feeds as an option, and considering that blogs are all about "conversation," being notified when something new has been said makes a lot of sense.

Build Your Own Feed

In the not-too-distant future, we expect to see blogs that offer feed "wizards" that will permit readers to mix and match syndication criteria as they see fit. We often visit sites where we want to create a customized feed using specific category, author, and/or keywords as criteria.

Although not a blog per se, programmers at Apple have integrated RSS feeds into their music application iTunes, and offer great flexibility to their subscribers. With the iTunes service, you can subscribe to feeds for new releases, top-ten songs, and more.

One of the few drawbacks to offering many different "flavors" of feeds (and why hosted services tend to avoid them) is that it can tax the computers that serve up your blog(s). Thousands of readers receiving hundreds of customized content streams could stress your servers as they work overtime trying to keep up when you add new content.

Not only can customizable feeds make life easier for your readers, they can also make you money. In the next section, we'll talk about how making special modifications to your pages and feeds can attract advertisers and sponsors.

Ads on Your Blog

While blogs can be useful as an enhancement to your business, sometimes your blog can *be* the business.

The primary ways bloggers can earn income from their sites are via advertising and sponsorships, and there are more than a few who are making a good living from these sources.

The good news is that adding revenue-generating features like ads to your blog is very easy. The not-so-good news is that your site will need to be extremely popular for the revenue to be more than trivial. Even though riches are hard to come by, many bloggers are happy just to make enough to cover their hosting costs.

Ad Services for Bloggers

More and more advertisers are moving their ad dollars away from traditional media (television and print advertising) to online publications and blogs; this trend is working in bloggers' favor. In 2005, *Advertising Age* reported that the combined advertising revenues of Google and Yahoo! are rivaling the combined prime-time ad revenues of ABC, CBS, and NBC. The Internet has clearly become the fastest-growing advertising medium.

Sponsorships are another method that can provide bloggers with compensation for their efforts. Creating a blog that aligns with a target audience can be attractive to a corporate sponsor. Many companies are eager to have an ongoing branding presence on a well-executed blog. We have sites that garner revenues from both ads and sponsorships and can confirm what many bloggers say—sponsorships are generally more lucrative and make for a better experience for their visitors.

Some sponsored sites include Vespa Blog (*www.vespablog.com*, sponsored by Piaggio USA), Real Baking with Rose (*www.realbakingwithrose.com*, sponsored by Gold Medal Flour), and our own inFlightHQ (sponsored by Connexion by Boeing).

How Ads Work

If you have a popular blog, there are literally dozens of companies that will eagerly work with you to host ads and compensate you for your online real estate. Even if your site is not hugely popular, there are still several ad networks that will administer an advertising campaign on your blog.

Getting ads up on your blog can be a very simple process. All you have to do is sign up to participate in some kind of online ad network and they'll provide you with HTML or scripting code that you then insert onto your page template or Web server. Once that is in place, small text ads will start appearing, people will start clicking, and (with a little luck) the checks will start coming in.

The most popular ad service that bloggers of all kinds use is Google's AdSense network. AdSense subscribers are paid based on how many visitors click on the ads Google presents on your pages. After filling out an application at the AdSense site, Google will likely approve you and will then route you to a page that lets you specify how you want your ads to look (note that you can't specifically control what ads appear, but can filter out your competitors and phrases).

Next, you will be provided with proper ad code to insert into your blog. Once that code is in place, the ads will be fed into your blog.

After your ads have been up and running for a few hours, you can then go to your AdSense account page and watch how many people have seen the ads (these views are called *impressions*), how many people have clicked on ads, and most importantly, how many dollars have been credited to you.

There are several other ad networks that work similarly. Yahoo! offers one, Kanoodle is another, and more are cropping up all the time. Kanoodle is integrated into some hosted services such as TypePad, which makes signing up even simpler for users of those networks.

When choosing a pay-per-click ad network, you want to make sure that it has features that make ad placements highly relevant to your readers. This will ensure that your ads get more clicks. AdSense and Yahoo! are the leaders in this arena. As we reviewed the various services, we learned that some can't do things like geographic targeting, or even base ads on keyword analysis. These are capabilities that both AdSense and Yahoo! offer.

For click ad networks like AdSense, revenues are affected by several factors, including how many visitors you get to your site, where ads are positioned, the likelihood of people to click, and what advertisers are paying Google for clicks (ads for Viagra cost advertisers more than ads for chewing gum). As a rough reference point, one digital photography blog we work with gets about 600 visitors a day (moderate traffic), their ad network places camera-related ads prominently (moderate cost to advertisers), and averages about $50 a month worth of click revenue to the blogger.

You can also host ads for a flat rate based on time. Some popular advertising networks such as BlogAds allow you to set your own price for advertisers to place ads of various sizes and positions on your pages. You then pay the BlogAds service a percentage of all revenues received.

Ads on RSS Feeds

An emerging blog-centric source for Internet advertising income is from
RSS ad placements. A few of the same networks that will put ads on your
pages will also put promotions into your feeds.

This means that people who read your posts in their newsreaders (but don't
visit your site) can still be "monetized." This type of placement is still in the
early stages of development, but the importance of this ad genre will become
more and more relevant over time. We anticipate that a major slice of the
blog ad revenue pie will come from this source in the next few years.

As of this writing, Google is testing RSS ads as an optional feature for AdSense
partners. One of the pioneers in this space, FeedBurner (*www.feedburner.com*)
will not only compensate you for ads in your feeds, but will also provide
detailed tracking of how many people are subscribing to your syndicated
content, along with readership statistics.

One of the drawbacks of FeedBurner and most other RSS ad services is
that in a strict sense, visitors will not actually be subscribing to "your" feeds.
Instead, they will be subscribing to FeedBurner feeds that contain your
content. This means that should you decide to discontinue using an RSS
ad service (or switch to another one), all of your current subscribers will be
"orphaned" and will no longer receive your posts. You'll have to redirect
them to another feed.

If you have installed blogging software on your own server (versus using a
hosted service), a plug-in or script that allows you to place your own ads into
the RSS stream is likely to be available. This means you can advertise your
own products or sell space in your feeds to other organizations.

Some Internet purists loathe the notion of advertising sullying the purity of
RSS content, and inserting ads may generate negative comments from some.
Gawker Media has an innovative approach to this. They offer two types of
feeds: Partial (subject line and some introductory text) with no ads, or full
(the complete post) with RSS ads inserted.

Sponsorship Deals

Sometimes advertisers will approach you in hopes of being the sole commercial presence on the blog, and may want you to occasionally profile their products or services within your posts. In some cases, you may even be approached to create a brand new blog dedicated to a target market. Depending on how much posting effort you can commit to and how much visibility or "buzz" you can generate for the blog, revenues can range from slightly more than AdSense income to several thousand dollars a month.

> **NOTE:** If you do become a paid blogger, be sure to disclose that you're being paid and by whom. More than one blogger has been exposed for accepting payments and not disclosing it, and nothing will sink a blog faster than being unethical.

One documented example of this was Sony's sponsorship of the LifeHacker blog. Sony paid the site, part of the Gawker Media network, $25,000 a month for three months to be the sole advertiser; editorial content was not affected. While this sounds like something to pursue, don't quit your day job yet. This type of compensation is unlikely for the lone blogger, one who doesn't host a network of popular sites. One reason Sony likely went with Gawker Media is that they have a highly trafficked network. Being able to feature mentions and links from those other blogs back into the LifeHacker site could provide significant search engine visibility for LifeHacker and Sony.

Ad Strategies

As with other marketing-related blogging initiatives, the main strategic goal is for your blog to have lots of visitors, readers, and inbound links. If your site has those things going for it, any ad or sponsorship program you administer will be much more lucrative. High-level strategies for increasing traffic and links will be covered in depth in Chapter 7, "Launching Your Blog and Getting Noticed." But there are some basic tactical approaches that can help a blog get more advertising revenues.

The first is that familiar mantra: location, location, location. Where you locate pay-per-click ads on your pages is critical. Using the eye-tracking map we presented in Chapter 4 can help you place your ads where they'll get the most visibility. In addition, there are ways to place these ads at the top or bottom of individual posts. One blogger we know who makes thousands of dollars a month from AdSense ads claims that placing ads midpost results in the most clicks.

Being topical with your posts can also help drive an increase in traffic to your site and can likely result in more people clicking on your ads. We've discovered that posts covering "hot" topics like the iPod, or perhaps a just-released Harry Potter movie can result in a temporary surge of visits and ad clicks. As long as you can remain topical and true to your blog's mission, this strategy can effectively drive additional ad revenue without sacrificing your editorial focus.

Although not for everyone, ads and sponsorships can be a handy way to help defer the costs of blogging, and with luck can provide some healthy revenue.

If your site generates a lot of traffic, and you don't mind having precious onscreen real estate taken up by small virtual "billboards," you should investigate this option.

Bear in mind that features and tools are in a constant state of flux and improvement, so some of the specifics we've presented in this chapter may have changed. Software and services are updated constantly, and third-party enhancements are being created everyday.

The good news is that the fundamentals of hosted, installed, and enterprise tools will likely remain fairly static for some time. Also, the information we present here will allow those new to blogging to perform intelligent research into features and capabilities they want.

In Chapter 6, "Writing Your Blog," we'll get into the most important thing to do after you get your system up and running—start writing!

Writing Your Blog

When it comes to blogging, the writing is where the proverbial rubber meets the road. You can have the best software, the fastest servers, and a fabulous team of experts, but if you're not posting the right things, the right way, at the right time, you'll be at a serious disadvantage.

In this chapter, we focus on how to take the tools at your disposal and align them with your skills and talents so that you can create killer content that gets attention and respect.

Passion and Purpose

The best blogs, the ones that get a lot of readers and buzz, have authors who are passionate about their sites and are dedicated to creating great online destinations. Passionate and purposeful blogs are built on three pillars of success: they are regularly updated; they have excellent content; and they deliver value for their intended audience. Understanding how these pillars work together is critical to having not just a good blog, but a great one.

Commitment to Content

Put a dozen successful bloggers in a room, and in short order the debates will begin over the thorny issues of the blogosphere. Are partial feeds evil? How should comments be moderated (if at all)? Do tags matter? And so on. In fact, you'll find that there are few things that experienced bloggers universally agree on. One of the rare items that would be largely undisputed among this group is that authors should be committed to providing their audiences with information that matters, and they should create content that will make their readers want to come back.

Influential bloggers with a large and dedicated readership know that staying aligned with this directive will not only make their readers happy, but it can also mean lots of traffic. Over time, it can also help a blogger attain a position of "thought leadership" which, as we mentioned in Chapter 2, "Determining Your Focus," is a primary reason many people decide to blog in the first place.

Commitment to content means understanding that posting is now an integral part of your life. It means you'll want to constantly scan the horizon for items to write about, and to figure out how to make those items relevant to your readers. Later in this chapter, we'll discuss specific methods that can help you create a virtual "lookout tower" to help you find appropriate items as they emerge.

If providing compelling content is a strategy for success, the key tactic is to focus on bringing something new to the table. The blogosphere is often criticized for being an "echo chamber" because so much material is repeated and linked to over and over without any expansion, enhancement, or insight.

A study conducted at the University of California, Berkeley in 2005 confirms that blog readers prefer new material to echo chamber content. The report said that "Participants overwhelmingly commented that a good post is one that contributes new information or, to a lesser extent, extensive commentary about some issue on which the participant is an expert."

You'll often see posts that say things like "Gern Blanston has posted today about how corporate governance has suddenly become a major issue for the hamster breeding industry." Compare that to a post that reads "Gern may have missed the mark with his post. I found this 1998 interview with a former CFO of Hamsterco yesterday, and he said way back then that there was a crisis emerging...." The former is what we call "regurgitorial"; the latter enhances and expands. Instead of "check this out, there's an interesting article about vacationing on Maui," try "This article mentions one of our favorite restaurants in Maui. If you go there, try to get a table on the balcony, as it has a great sunset view." If you refer to an existing post, enhance and expand—don't regurgitate.

Better yet, when practical, try to create posts that are not derived from other blog writings at all. There's an old saying to write what you know—and chances are you know a lot about your business.

Use your unique personal experience and knowledge to create original content that *others* can regurgitate.

Posting for Your Audience

Blogging began as a platform where authors would write posts covering whatever topics interested them, and they drew visitors that were attracted by those postings. In this author-centric model, the blogger writes for himself and doesn't particularly consider specific audience needs. The nice thing about this model is that when bloggers write about their own interests, they tend to write more often, and with more passion. The other advantage is that there is a natural alignment between writer and audience.

With business blogs, there is a much greater chance that audience-targeting considerations will come into play. In Chapter 1, "Meet the Blogs," we described several different types of blogs that businesses should consider, and those clearly strive to serve a particular set of readers. If you are looking to attract a specific audience, writing whatever you feel like may not be the best solution.

It seems intuitive that understanding what your target wants, and tailoring your writing to better serve them, is a good idea. As the newspaper industry knows well, it's also a strategy that can increase your readership. Studies by the Readership Institute at Northwestern University have shown that newspapers that focus on understanding and meeting the needs of their reading customers perform better. As the institute reported in their 2002 Impact Study of Readership, "There was a clear and strong linkage—as newspapers became more reader-oriented, their readership also tended to rise."

For decades, publications of all sorts have worked to understand their readers better. Surveys, focus groups, and interviews are all effective tools in this effort. Surveying services like Zoomerang.com and Surveymonkey.com have helped us to better understand what our audience values, and thanks to traffic monitoring tools like Mint and Google Analytics, we can see what posts get the most clicks. (Traffic will be discussed in Chapter 8, "Monitoring and Managing Your Blog.")

Bloggers have a powerful tool at their disposal that most other publications and Web sites do not. Comments attached directly to posts provide critiques and compliments that can guide future efforts. As the bloggers at TamsPalm (*http://tamspalm.tamoggemon.com*), a blog covering the Palm OS, said in 2005, "Hundreds of anonymous comments helped us evolve and improve our content and coverage." Even if people don't comment on your site, blog search engines such as Technorati, PubSub, and Google Blog Search make it easy to discover what others are saying about your posts on their own sites.

TIP: Don't let your blog be guided solely by comments. Comments are just one factor to your blog; it's most important to have strong ideas, ethos, and to be yourself.

A tactic that bloggers might consider is one that other publications have used effectively for years. The development of an editorial "advisory board" can assist in the development of better-targeted posts. In addition, picking visible, influential members of that board can lend some promotional value to the process. We employed this technique when we launched the Blog Business Summit, and it clearly helped us create better content, and drove traffic.

Posting Frequently

Bloggers with passion and purpose are constantly adding new content to their sites. Experienced blog authors know that the more often you post, the more attention your blog will receive. One of the reasons for this is that Google notices how often sites are updated, and factors this in when deciding how relevant a site is. All other things being equal, a blog that gets posted to several times a day will rank much higher than a blog that receives new content once a week. Google also focuses its attention on the subject lines in blog posts, so the more unique subject lines you introduce into the blogosphere, the more searches you'll be listed in.

This is why you'll see a lot of short posts on many of the more popular blogger sites. These bloggers tend to break longer articles into shorter, more focused posts. For example, if you were going to write a long piece about a new product you were developing, you might instead break it into several posts covering market analysis, working with the designers, engineering a prototype, going into production, and so on. As a general rule, try to break your topics into the smallest bite-size chunks possible. Not only does this encourage search engines to list your site, it also fits with the way that readers interact with the Web.

Blogger Jeffrey Zeldman learned the hard way that not posting can affect traffic. Zeldman (*www.zeldman.com*), who publishes A List Apart, stopped updating his personal site with new articles for several weeks and found the traffic drop to be stunning. Eventually, the site was redesigned and rolled out with new articles with frequent updates and has enjoyed a triumphant return to being a heavily trafficked destination. To prevent a drop-off in visits, many bloggers hire or ask other bloggers to "baby-sit" their blog while they work on other projects (like a book) or go on vacation.

While there are no hard and fast rules for what is the optimal posting frequency (and Google does not reveal how it factors site updating), an analysis of the posting frequency of the top 100 blogs as tracked by Technorati shows that the average number of posts per day is between five and six. A number of bloggers who have adjusted their posting frequency and analyzed the resulting traffic numbers claim three posts a week is a minimum, and three times a day is where you begin to see some serious traffic. The best guideline of all may be the one put forth by Buzz Bruggeman, who claims that you need to be posting "more often than your closest competitor."

With passion and purpose, your blog can be a labor of love that meets pragmatic business goals. Understanding what's required and using the many tools at your disposal, there's no reason that you can't achieve the success of an "A list" blogger. As with so many ventures in life, enthusiasm and commitment can make all the difference.

Starting the Conversation

If there's a single word we see associated more often than any other with the word *blog,* it's *conversation.* In the 2001 book *The Cluetrain Manifesto,* Doc Searls and David Weinberger advocated that businesses should stop treating online communities as "targets" and proposed instead that "markets are conversations."

Many serious business bloggers firmly believe their companies need to "get on the Cluetrain," and many have created blogs that are not only designed to invoke discussion on the Web, they are also almost exclusively written in a conversational style.

Engaging readers and inspiring them to get involved by commenting or linking is likely to be your goal. Having a clear, authentic, and approachable style is a great way to make that happen.

Authentic and Conversational

If you want to truly engage your readers, you'll want to avoid the type of writing that has been the staple of corporate marketing and PR departments for years. The stilted "corpspeak" common to press releases and big business home pages will generally not be as well received by your readers as much as less formal copy with a more genuine voice.

There are several reasons that authentic, conversational copy makes sense. One of the best reasons is that it's just good writing. As a primer, we suggest that you read *The Elements of Style* by William Strunk and E. B. White. They advise writers to avoid "all mannerisms, tricks, adornments." Instead they advocate "plainness, simplicity, orderliness, sincerity." In *On Writing Well*, William Zinsser says, "Good writers are always visible just behind their words."

Another reason to adopt a conversational approach is that it will likely help you and your organization create a stronger relationship with your readers. A human voice not only intuitively seems like a way to bond with your audience, there's also concrete evidence backing up that assertion. In 2006, a study at the School of Journalism and Mass Communication at the University of North Carolina at Chapel Hill confirmed that corporate blogs tended to impart a "conversational human voice" on an organization, and that "perceived relational strategies (conversational human voice, communicated relational commitment) were found to correlate significantly with relational outcomes (trust, satisfaction, control mutuality, commitment)." In other words, blogs written in a conversational voice can help corporations forge positive relationships with customers.

Conversational writing is not really the same as conversational speech. Writers still need to carefully craft what they write, and edit their copy thoroughly. The nature of conversational writing is really one of style. Conversational style is informal (avoids jargon and flowery language), inviting (friendly, prompts for feedback), transparent (candid, not promotional), direct (gets to the point), and engaging (invokes a sense of humor).

Compare "We discovered that the most prevalent cause of processor-based system failure involved read/write head engagement issues" to "Most computer breakdowns are caused by bad hard drives." One is cumbersome and hard to interpret; the other is conversational, clear, and easy to understand.

To learn how to write conversationally, you should start reading a bunch of blogs to get a sense of others' style. Check out ALA's articles on writing (*http://www.alistapart.com/articles/writebetter*) and consider that blogging is like sending an email to the world. It's likely that your email voice, the one you use when you write to your friends, is the right voice for your blog.

Having reference books (like Strunk & White) on hand is important, especially if you're unsure about your grammar skills. If you are unsure about your writing, the best way to learn is to start posting a lot. D. Keith Robinson's audience (*www.7nights.com/asterisk/*) helped him learn to write better by offering suggestions and even editing his grammar and spelling!

When we write lengthy posts, we'll spell and grammar check them in Word to make sure we didn't miss anything obvious. We also share posts with each other, as drafts, and ask for feedback.

In his article, "How to Write a Better Weblog," Dennis A. Mahoney observed, "In 1994, you could hook a thousand readers (to your blog) if you wrote about the mold underneath your refrigerator. Now, you're lucky to get a hundred regulars, even if your work is excellent." The key is to write as if your readers were paying you and compel them to subscribe to your RSS feed. In order to do that, you've got to have something to say—and you've got to say it clearly.

Interesting and Expressive

One of the key reasons blogs became so popular in the early days had nothing to do with Google, RSS feeds, or any techie underpinnings. Both then and now, people read blogs because they express a personal experience. Blogs can provide an insider's view, and that opens up a world not served by traditional journalism. This is the type of writing that readers seek out and embrace. Even if you don't end up with millions of page views a year, you can open up your business and express yourself in a way that draws the reader in.

Expressive writers tap into their experiences and use anecdotes, humor, and emotion to make their personalities come alive in their writings. They take the time to use words that capture what they really feel, and avoid generalities. Was the evening merely "great" (yawn), or did it remind you of summer nights on the porch when you were a kid?

We're not advising writers to delve into mundane details of their everyday lives (no one likely cares about what your cat had for breakfast), but try to give your readers a sense of who you are.

The most popular blogs often have a lot of personality. Some have heavy doses of bombast (*www.andrewsullivan.com*), and others even delve into their sex lives (*www.washingtonienne.com/blog.html*). While most business blogs shouldn't be tell-all expose sites, it's okay for posts to be somewhat provocative (while keeping within company guidelines). Readers engage with a writer when they feel they know them as more than just an information transmission medium.

Many of the most popular tech blogs contain posts about vacations, dinners out, and other personal experiences of the authors. Feel free to interject some of these into the mix if it fits your style.

Try to put healthy doses of you into what you write. Readers will thank you for it, and you'll find the job of writing much easier.

Brief and to the Point

Less is more. Long-winded posts are the hallmark of the amateur writer. Good bloggers strive for simplicity. Less copy not only makes it easier for your readers to understand your main points quickly and easily, but it also makes the job of writing easier.

A great way to ensure that you write with brevity is to take the time to review and trim copy before you take posts live. We often stop and remove words systematically until a passage "breaks." Words and phrases that should be avoided include: "basically," "due to the fact that," "whether or not," "exhibit a tendency to." Any words that don't add to the meaning should be deleted.

Compare these two sentences:

- "Make sure you select blog software that contains community-oriented features that allow for a back-and-forth dialog between author and reader."

- "Buy software that has commenting features."

As you can see, careful pruning can make a big difference.

A good blogger is conversational, concise, and makes sure his or her writings convey a sense of who they are. If your personal writing style is something you are still trying to determine, we suggest that you take time to read other blogs and get a feel for what approaches might best align with your personality. The more you read, the better you'll be at writing.

Making an Impression

Even the greatest writing in the world won't be of much value if no one gets to read it. If you take into consideration the factors that affect how findable your posts are, you'll see your readership grow.

There are several techniques that can increase the likelihood that people will find you when they search, as well as choose your writings over others.

Writing Findable Content

When striving for maximum readership, one of the most critical choices you can make is how you decide to title your posts. Search engines weight the subject lines that appear at the top of each entry heavily, and RSS newsreaders typically display titles only unless a reader double-clicks to read further.

For those reasons, smart bloggers take the time to select words and phrases that will match searches that they expect their target audience to make. They also attempt to write subject lines that will compel subscribers to read further.

The easy way to meet both goals is to avoid cryptic, vague, and/or cute subject lines. Subject lines like "check this out," "what do you think," and "wazzzup," don't align with searchers' needs and are likely not compelling enough for many to want to read more. Phrases that combine the best of both worlds might be ones like "My iPod is Haunted," "How I find cheap airline fares," or "Getting a job interview at Google."

The first paragraphs of your entries are weighted more heavily by search engines than paragraphs that come later, so you'll want to try to introduce relevant terms early in your posts. In Chapter 7, "Launching Your Blog and Getting Noticed," we'll talk more about how to identify search keywords that might be relevant to your audience.

Lots of Links

One of the policies we've established for our blogs is that all posts must contain at least one outbound link. For some, this notion might seem silly—why would you give a visitor an easy way to leave your site and go to another? One old-school computer trade press manager we know had what we called a "cul-de-sac" policy: no linking out. His idea was that the sites his company hosted should not promote any method of departure. What's telling is that one of his former employees is now a blogger whose site has focused almost exclusively on outbound links. This blogger's site is now far more visible than his previous employer's online network of cyber "roach motels."

There are many reasons why linking out from your site makes good sense and is in your best interest. One reason is that evidence suggests that Google likes sites that link judiciously to pages on other sites, especially to sites that Google has deemed to be "authorities." Another reason is that outbound links can be a way for your site to get noticed. Many bloggers monitor their referrer logs religiously, and when clicks come in from your site, they'll likely notice it. These bloggers may comment and/or link back to you in response. It's also a courteous thing to do, and marks you as a respectful member of the blogging community.

The best reason may be that good links provide value to your readers. Links can clarify or support a position you've taken, which permits a reader to learn more. A link to a valuable resource, along with a helpful description, can also be a reason for a new visitor to subscribe to your feed, or ask to join your email list.

Being Provocative

If there's one thing we know about blog writing, it's that our provocative posts get more clicks, links, and comments than our more benign writings. Controversy is a great way to start a vigorous conversation, and to get people thinking. When appropriate, we encourage all bloggers to use thoughtful provocation to drive attention.

Provocative doesn't mean combative. Some bloggers have made a career out of being snarky and spend much of their time being belligerent just to get attention. Like spoiled children, they typically take a combative stance on just about everything, and their writings are effused with negativity and can frequently be insulting. Don't be that guy.

Being provocative can be done in a positive way. Sometimes just asking a question can get the ball rolling, such as "Hey, business blog x has turned off comments—is that the best way to deal with spam?" Simply reporting certain facts can also drive robust discussion. When we blogged about the fact that the phrase "Robert Scoble" typed into Google yielded many more mentions than typing in the name of one of the world's top PR firms, readers took notice. One had been blogging for a few years; the other had issued thousands of press releases for decades. Many readers stepped up to say things such as "PR firms are there to publicize clients, not themselves," and that "Google mentions are not all that accurate." We loved it. The more people talked, the more traffic and links we received.

Don't be a wallflower at the party. Bring up topics that get people involved and interested. Get the debate fired up. Your readers will thank you for it, and your presence in the blogosphere will be enhanced.

One blogger got fed up with voice mail hell and created an online "cheat sheet" that provides shortcuts to get you through to a human when calling for service or support at dozens of companies. His site (*www.gethuman.com*) became hugely popular thanks to his provocative stance countering the big corporations' intentions.

Just a few simple strategies can yield powerful benefits in terms of readership and prominence. Focusing on how searchers and subscribers make choices, along with careful consideration of what will drive conversation, can ensure that your blog isn't lost in the crowd.

Posting Process

The heart and soul of blogging is posting, and the better you are at it, the better your blog will be. While all bloggers are different, and each has a unique style, there are a few common tools and techniques that can give you an edge in the posting process.

Watch Your Space

The great bloggers seem to have a sixth sense for capturing the latest information relevant to their subject areas. Being consistently first with important information can give you an edge over other Web sites, and the best bloggers know the tricks for staying on top of breaking news. There are hundreds of tools and techniques for knowing what's going on in your market space, but here are the essentials that can give you an immediate edge.

Most importantly is to start using some kind of RSS newsreader software or service immediately. Your newsreader will serve as the customized central "dashboard" into which all the information you've asked to receive will flow. Your newsreader will assimilate the RSS feeds that you have subscribed to, and present them all in one place. The top bloggers use Web sites like Bloglines (*www.bloglines.com*, see **Figure 6.1**) or software programs like NewsGator for the PC or NetNewsWire for the Mac as their central information dashboard. There are many dozens of other programs and sites that can manage subscriptions, including all the major Web browsers.

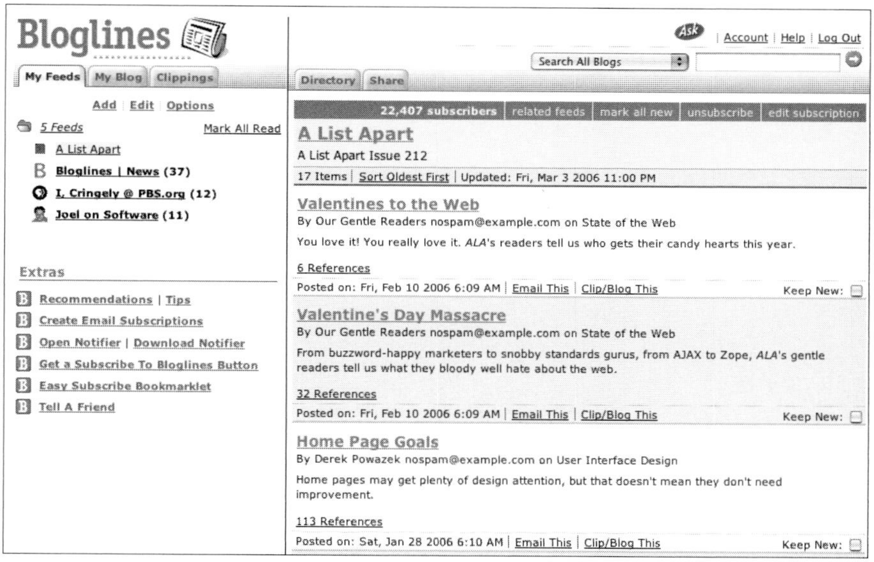

Figure 6.1

Bloglines is a popular online newsreader that can manage subscriptions from any site that generates syndicated feeds.

One benefit of using a Web-based service like Bloglines is that you can access your feeds from different computers and locations—like using a Hotmail or Yahoo! email account. Others prefer to run a desktop application because they want access to the information even when they're not online. If you get on a plane and you boot up NewsGator, all of your most recently downloaded feeds will be available to read. If you try to log into Bloglines at 30,000 feet, you're out of luck (unless you have in-flight Internet!). Another benefit of using desktop newsreader applications is that you can run specific filtering operations on downloaded feeds. For example, NetNewsWire can search through thousands of downloaded feeds and further filter them for keywords. Imagine you have subscribed to dozens of wine blogs and want to be alerted when one of them mentions "Walla Walla." This is easy with a desktop application.

Okay, so you have your newsreader up and running, and can now aggregate all of these RSS feeds. The big question now is what feeds should you be receiving? This is where it gets interesting. A complete understanding of all the ways to subscribe to information can provide you with a treasure trove of relevant information. There are literally millions of feeds available; here are the three broad categories that you can subscribe to:

Subscribe to site feeds. When you find a relevant blog (or other site that features RSS feeds), subscribe to it in your newsreader. Unless a site indicates otherwise, this kind of subscription will automatically funnel all new information published on that site into your newsreader.

Subscribe to blog/RSS searches. Much of the power of feed reading comes from receiving results from searches of other blogs. You're probably already using search engines like Google or Yahoo!, and they're useful for finding answers to specific questions, but the problem is that there's no easy way to be alerted when new matching items appear. If you want to know every time Google picks up a competitor mention, you're largely out of luck.

Fortunately, there are specialized blog search engines where you can input searches and then capture the results as RSS feeds that will be automatically updated in your newsreader as new items appear. Search sites like Technorati, PubSub, Feedster, and others scan blogs (and other sites that provide feeds) and then let you subscribe to these searches. Although a bit late to the game, Google has now created their own special blog search engine (*www.blogsearch. google.com/*), and their search results can also be subscribed to as a feed. As of this writing, they do not offer a free method to subscribe to search results from their main search page.

Subscribe to non-syndicated content. You can subscribe to all RSS information from specific blogs, and you can subscribe to searches of RSS content, but there is a massive amount of information on the Web that is not normally subscribable. Wouldn't it be nice if you could easily receive updated content that isn't syndicated? Luckily there are ways to have information that's not normally available via RSS appear in your newsreader.

Google and Yahoo! both have search pages that are dedicated to news, and are constantly scanning newspapers, television, and other sources for breaking stories. Many of the things they find are not coming from RSS feeds, but the searches you can make on these pages can be subscribed to as a feed. This is where you can enter a competitor's name and automatically receive all of their breaking press releases in your newsreader. Alas, Google and Yahoo! News won't catch when a non-news Web site mentions a company, but it's still a great way to get a lot of relevant information.

Few people know that Microsoft's MSN search engine will let you save their general searches as feeds. This means you can receive updates on subjects from non-blog sites as they appear within their search engine. We use MSN quite a bit for this reason. It's not perfect, as you will see items get repeated over time, but it's an excellent way to get information that other bloggers aren't tuned in to.

Posting Tools

In Chapter 5, "Tools and Implementation," we introduced the idea of using a desktop blog editor to help you compose posts and manage your content even when offline. For many of the most prolific bloggers, a desktop blogging tool is a must, not only for the reasons we described earlier, but also because several of them can integrate directly with a variety of newsreaders. This integration can provide huge advantages for those bloggers who want to post frequently and strive to provide the freshest content.

When a feedreader and a posting application can talk to each other, it means that you can quickly and easily take an interesting article or post you've discovered and implant it into your own blog with your comments and insights. This seamless transfer can replace a cumbersome sequence of copying and pasting between multiple applications. Within seconds, you can create a new post based on information that just landed on your desktop.

We use the combination of NetNewsWire (newsreader) and Ecto (desktop editor, see **Figure 6.2**) to quickly transfer the freshest information into new posts on any and all of our sites.

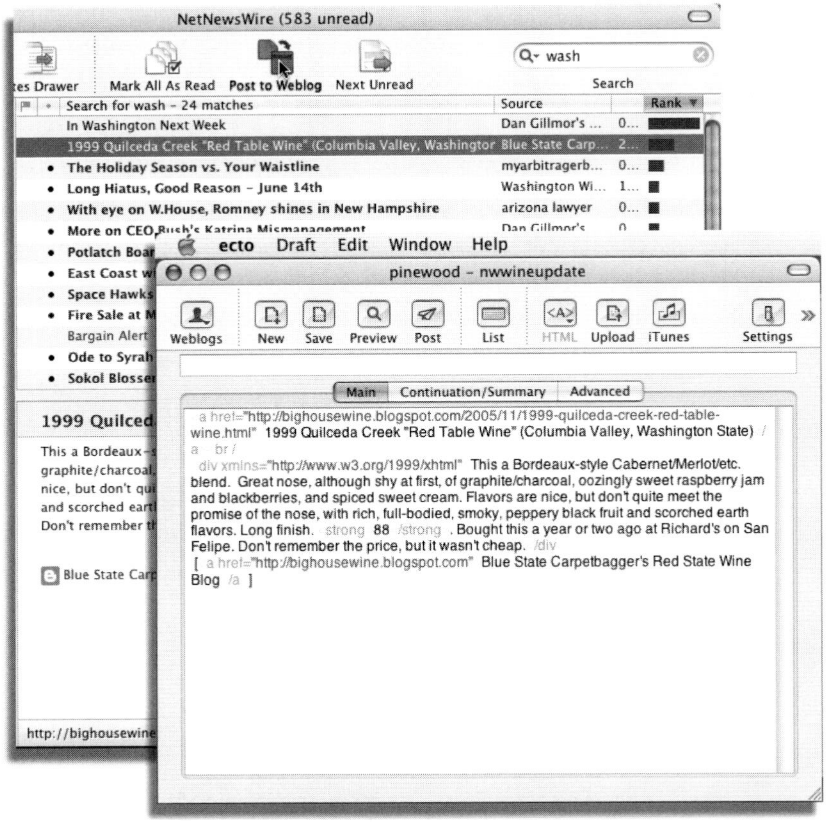

Figure 6.2

Any post viewed in NetNewsWire can be transferred automatically into several blog editors, including Ecto.

Other possible combinations include linking incoming posts from NewsGator and FeedDemon (both excellent newsreaders) into BlogJet (a highly rated desktop blog editor).

Since there are dozens of possible newsreaders and editors to choose from and the linkages are not uniform, we suggest that you first research news-readers to see which ones have the features you want. Then you can investigate further to see what editors they align with. This information should be available on the Web sites of the newsreaders you're studying.

KEEP THE CODE CLEAN

We've described how the clean standards-compliant HTML that blog engines use to create their pages offers many advantages over the sites built from traditional HTML and other database-driven methods. Having code that Google finds attractive and that can be easily read in a myriad of devices (cell phones, PDAs, screen readers) opens up a vast audience that other sites can't easily reach.

For years, we've urged our clients and the audiences at our events not to mess up a great thing by putting "garbage" HTML code into the posts they write. While it's true that inserting HTML code into the text of your posts can add formatting that can enhance readability, often that HTML will be non-standard.

For example, much of the HTML Microsoft Word creates is non-compliant and will overpower the clean HTML that Google respects so much. In addition, it can eliminate the ability for a post to be read in browsers and devices that aren't using Windows Internet Explorer. Our advice is to use Word for composing and for spelling and grammar checking, but don't use the formatting options. In fact, we generally copy and paste from Word into programs that deal with straight text only and then copy that into our blog engines or editors.

Pasting Word text into programs like Text Edit or BBEdit on the Mac, or using clipboard utilities like Clip Strip for Windows can convert formatted copy into clean trouble-free plain text. Another way to ensure that no residual Word formatting is inserted is to save your Word doc to the plain text format (using a .txt extension) and copy and paste the text from there into your blog authoring tool.

If you aren't an HTML jockey, and want bold, italics, or other formatting controls, use the options available in either your blog engine or in your editor (Ecto, BlogJet, etc.). These tools tend to create the clean HTML needed to stay compliant.

Time to Blog

As we've said many times, frequent, timely posts that prompt conversation can propel your site into the limelight. At the root of it all is posting. You have to do it, and (as with all things in life) if you dedicate both time and an effective system toward that process, you'll be a success.

Finding the time to blog can be a challenge, and even many of the high-visibility bloggers find it tough to squeeze in several posts a day. Many say that if you religiously schedule an hour or two daily toward research and posting, you'll be able to achieve the momentum required. Many find that early mornings or late nights provide for quality blogging time. Whatever your schedule permits, a focused set of minutes, or hours, each day dedicated toward monitoring, reflection, and writing will serve you well.

The specifics of how you work is up to you, but here is a process to blogging that works for us and many others.

Begin by taking inventory of comments that have come in. You may need to respond, or a reader may have provided a link for you to investigate or expand upon. Your readers are the heart and soul of the blog conversation and will often give you great leads to follow up on.

Next, review your email. A significant amount of relevant material can come in from the friends, family, and associates sending articles your way. We save these tidbits into a special folder for retrieval when it's time to get posting. Even emails containing non-public information may yield insights that can lead to informative posts. As your blog becomes popular, you'll find that your readers will send you related items to post on.

Peruse those few key sites that contain information vital to your editorial arena that don't issue RSS feeds. If you are a regular visitor, and discover new material there, there is a chance that it hasn't been posted on yet, and you can have a blogosphere "scoop." We love those sites that the other bloggers aren't paying close attention to.

At this stage, you may have identified some time-sensitive items that should be blogged about ASAP. If you have, get those up immediately. If not, continue on to gather more possible editorial fodder.

Next, take some time to review your traffic stats. You may discover that clicks are coming in from a source that you hadn't been aware of. Knowing who is talking about you, and gathering some insights from a visit to their site can provide you with unforeseen editorial ideas.

Then review your newsreader for the latest updates. Most of these applications have features that allow you to flag items for posting, so you can sweep through many entries and set aside those that you want to come back to later. It's not unreasonable to filter out hundreds of items an hour, so depending on how much time you dedicate, it's conceivable that you can peruse the contents of several hundred Web sites in one day.

Applying a systematic approach to your posting can provide a means for you to write more and better posts each day. While you should not necessarily adopt our specific method to your individual process, we hope that you find a few helpful tips here that you can apply where appropriate.

A REAL TIMESAVER

If you want to save a lot of time and have more control over the formatting of the text you input, consider installing the Markdown with SmartyPants plug-in. It's widely available and will automatically create clean HTML formatting code as needed. One of the best things about Markdown with SmartyPants is that you can type simple formatting shorthand and the utility will convert it into more complex code for you. For example, if you type:

```
Click this [link](http://foo.com)
```

it will convert it to:

```
Click this <p><a href="http://foo.com">link</a></p>
```

List formatting, horizontal lines, line breaks, and many other features are all available using very simple text codes.

Engaging your audience with posts that bring something new to the conversation and dedicating your energies toward the writing process will reap dividends. After a few months of effort, you should begin to see your readership grow and your writing skill improve.

In Chapter 7, we'll cover some of the tricks of the trade for driving even more visitors and attention to your blog.

Launching Your Blog and Getting Noticed

It's getting harder and harder to make a splash in the blogosphere these days, because there's so much competition for reader interest. We've watched closely how other bloggers have been able to stand out from the rest of the pack, however, and there are specific tips and tricks to getting noticed and raking in the readership.

Many say that writing lots of great posts is enough to grab attention, but we're not convinced. We know from personal experience and from talking with other bloggers that more should be done.

The sections that follow apply to both brand-new blogs and old ones that have been around since the beginnings of the blogosphere.

Hit the Ground Running

As popular and effective as blogs are, you still can't just open your blog up for business and then sit back and wait for thousands of visitors and customers to arrive. The first successful blogs were the result of accidental entrepreneurship. This lucky accident no longer serves much purpose, and having a launch strategy is key.

Our launch-specific advice is to hit the ground running with a well designed and properly functioning blog (like we described in Chapter 4, "Designing for Readers"). Have several posts ready on your first day, asking for reader feedback. Respond quickly to comments to show you're listening and contributing to the conversation. A great example of a successful launch is the blog for Zillow (*www.zillowblog.com*), a real-estate site. On the day they launched their property-valuation site, they launched a blog with it to answer questions, explain how Zillow works, and introduce the people behind it. As their head of marketing said, "When we first decided to have a Zillow blog, we all agreed that this could be a powerful way to talk to people, hear from people, and engage in conversations with real customers using the site." Zillow was ready to engage the blogosphere, launched their blog, and by all measures it was a huge success.

Making It Interesting

The water cooler and the boardroom are both places where business people converge and exchange information. One is an informal hotbed of new developments and discussion—sometimes only tangentially related to office work—while the other is generally a more staid and often intimidating locale where less engaging content is the norm. We feel that it's best for bloggers to emulate the water cooler (if appropriate) because it provides a more interesting and attractive space.

Bringing Something New to the Party

Bloggers universally agree that posts covering new material tend to drive more interest and readership than writings derived from other posts. The problem is that coming up with fresh content on a regular basis can be a challenge. Many bloggers decide that the best way to provide unique material is to focus on personal experience. After all, your unique knowledge set and perspective can be what sets you apart from other bloggers.

For sites that are more industry- or market-focused, however, lots of personal stories may not be the way to go. Being first into the blogosphere with breaking news or other exclusive content can be essential. On every blog we publish, we work very hard to be the first to post about new developments that will interest our readership. When we do have "scoops," we see traffic surge.

One approach is to focus on finding source material that is not being readily fed into the RSS ecosystem. That can mean avoiding blogs, and news and magazine sites that offer syndicated feeds altogether. This is where your personal expertise comes in handy; you can probably find a treasure trove of sites that don't offer feeds in your area of interest. You should be the person to introduce those ideas to the blogosphere.

Note that we are not talking about "repurposing" or wholesale duplication of others' content. There are some "black-hat" bloggers that copy and paste entire writings without attribution, sometimes using automated systems that clone entire sites and slap ads onto them. These sites are the bane of the Web. The proper (and considerate) protocol is to write some brief commentary—perhaps quote small sections of these writings—and without exception link back to the original sources. If you can be the one to introduce interesting new sources to the feed readers of the world, and drive traffic in their direction, everyone wins.

After you have identified sources that don't syndicate, the next question is how can you get the latest information from them without having to constantly visit and scan those pages for new info? We've discovered that if you use the right tools, you can literally get RSS feeds that no one else in the world receives.

One solution is to pay for a subscription to Google Alert (not to be confused with Google Alerts) at *www.googlealert.com*. The service allows you to input search terms and receive new results as they appear in Google searches. We've found that combining this service with site-specific search requests (see sidebar) can yield targeted new content quite quickly. There can be as little as a one- to two-day delay between a site posting a new item and it appearing in your newsreader. There are drawbacks to Google Alert, however. Besides the cost, you will sometimes see old items that you've already reviewed reappear in the system flagged as new content.

SEARCHES WITHIN A WEB SITE: GETTING FEEDS NO ONE ELSE HAS

Experienced searchers know that you can have Google and MSN search within any site that it indexes. For example, at the Alaska Airlines Web site (*www.alaskaair.com*), there is no "search box" on their home page to help you find a specific item. Imagine you want to read their contract of carriage, and don't want to spend a bunch of time clicking around trying to find it. Try typing this into Google or MSN:

Carriage site: http://www.alaskaair.com

Voila! The search engine brings it right to you. Notice that in MSN (but not in Google), at the bottom of the page is a little orange RSS button. That means you can subscribe to this search and new entries that fit this query will appear in your newsreader automatically. While you may not want to get feeds about contracts of carriage, what about this search:

Promotion site: http://www.alaskaair.com

You have just created a feed that will notify you when a new page appears on the Alaska Airlines Web site containing the word *promotion*. Consider other possibilities. You could have MSN search a competitor's site for specific phrases and be automatically notified when they appear.

We've been impressed with the powerful "Feed for Free" service (*www.feed43.com*) that can derive RSS feeds from almost any Web site. It offers a way for you to indicate what headings are to be included in the feeds, and will send new headings and links into your newsreader as they appear. It can even save and recall searches from many forums and support sites. Using this service, we've been able to scoop other blogs because we have feeds they don't get. The only problem is that setting up new feeds is not for the non-techie. It requires some knowledge of HTML and an understanding of how Web pages are built.

Articles and reports from subscription-based sites are also handy sources of content that are not readily available to others. If you are lucky enough to have memberships or subscriptions that provide access to material unavailable to the general public, you may be able to bring some of it into the blogosphere. An even better source can be publications that don't put their material on the Web at all. If you get newsletters or print publications that are only paper-based, look for insights that might be of interest to your readers.

Providing Some Controversy

As we mentioned in Chapter 6, "Writing Your Blog," provocative posting can yield rewards. If you've spent some time listening to a few of the popular talk radio shows, you know there's a common thread that runs through them. The hosts of these highly trafficked media properties take firm positions on hotly debated issues. There is a similar situation on the Web. If you look at Technorati's list of top 100 bloggers, you'll see that most of the big names are far from being shy retiring types. A significant proportion of the most popular blogs such as Instapundit (*www.instapundit.com*), Daily Kos (*www.dailykos.com*), and The Huffington Post (*www.huffingtonpost.com*) are political sites, and their writers would be the first to say that they are not trying to be "objective" news sources. In fact, if you toss out the geek blogs covering technology issues, it's safe to say that most of the top 100 blogs have very opinionated content.

So if contrarian content can be effective in driving traffic and discussion, how do you meet your organizational/promotional needs and be "out there" at the same time? If you're blogging for Acme Widgets, what kind of posts can possibly incite discussion and avoid incurring the wrath of the higher-ups? One strategy is to consider your target audience and question some assumptions they hold.

Imagine that Acme Widgets has pinpointed a prime opportunity for new sales in the rapidly growing solar power industry. Posting about the anticipated exponential growth of solar as an energy source and what it might mean to the Middle East might drive some interesting discussion and debate.

Perhaps quoting an expert who believes Saudi Arabia will experience 20 percent unemployment as a result would bring in more links and traffic.

Another strategy that can instigate discussion at low risk is to refer to someone else's provocative post, especially if it's someone you'd like to link back to you.

Our experience backs up what other bloggers say about being appropriately controversial. Don't be shy, ask for feedback, and avoid long-winded posts. Put enough out there to get the discussion fired up, but don't provide a dissertation. A conversation is not the same as a lecture.

Knowing Your Readers

Successful blogging lies in getting new readers and having those readers come back for more. The more you know about your readers, the better chance you stand of delivering for them. The people who actually visit your site and/or subscribe to your posts may be different from the audience you had in mind originally, so it's a good idea to do what you can to get a better idea of precisely who is dropping by and why.

One of our clients is Colorado Ski Country. Their blogs go far beyond the brochureware of most ski resort Web sites. Several resort managers we spoke with told us that—more than anything—their visitors want to "feel like locals," which is something traditional market research had missed as a marketing opportunity. Their intimate understanding of their clients' needs enabled them to post on subjects that helped people be more a part of the resort community.

There are a variety of tools and techniques at your disposal that can help you get to know your audience better. Most of these methods are free or inexpensive, but require time and effort if you want to get useful results.

People who leave comments are a great resource. If you can keep the discussion going, try to learn more about who these visitors are, and why they came. You may want to email them in order to ask these questions. If you're new to the game and not receiving many comments yet, hang out at popular blogs that write about subjects similar to yours, and engage with people who comment frequently on those blogs.

Posting is about more than just providing meaty information. The best bloggers make sure there is some sizzle on the steak as well. Timely, targeted information that gets your audience involved can eventually get you the broad readership that will drive sales, enhance your corporate image, and help you achieve your other goals for the blogosphere.

Getting the Conversation Going

While posting is critical, it's tough to get a lot of attention when you're just getting started. With thousands of new blogs being created every day, you have to stand out in order to get a conversation going. Those new to blogging need to be aggressive and smart in order to get a dialog started.

Engaging the Blogosphere

One of the best ways to drive readership is to have other bloggers notice and link back to you. In fact, you can't have a truly successful blog without having that critical cross-pollination from other bloggers. Luckily, with a little time and effort, you can become a part of the conversation. You just need to take care not to do it in a ham-handed fashion.

If your goal is to get noticed by bloggers, you're not alone. Corporate clients and PR professionals frequently ask us "how can we pitch the bloggers?" We're happy that traditional marketers have recognized the influence of the blogosphere, but we cringe every time that question is posed. The quick answer is that you don't. *Pitching* is not the proper word for what needs to be done. A far more appropriate question is "how can I engage with the selected bloggers that our market trusts?"

This inappropriate focus on the "pitch" is one of the reasons that bloggers generally distrust the messages PR firms deliver. In a 2005 study conducted by Technorati, 821 bloggers were asked how much they trust messages sent from PR firms, on a scale of 1 to 10. The average response? A dismal 4.6.

We have watched many organizations reach out to the blogosphere in a myriad of ways, and have a pretty good feel for what works—and what doesn't. Whether you're trying to get bloggers interested in your products, or in your blogging efforts, here are few no-no's:

- Don't be indiscriminate. Carefully decide with whom you want to converse. It's far better to target the top 10 bloggers in your arena for engagement than annoy 1000 bloggers that were on somebody's email press list.

- Don't send messages that aren't tailored specifically to the blogger you're reaching out to. Do not send a generic email blast. Take the time to refer to a post they've made, or mention a common associate or other linkage.

- Don't send press releases. Most bloggers feel that being sent any marketing-speak whatsoever is an indicator of significant "cluelessness" on the part of the sender.

- Email is okay, but there are better options. Commenting on their blogs and writing your own blog posts that then link back to them creates open dialog, and resonates with bloggers.

If you take the time to consistently read the blogs that relate to your editorial or market arena, you'll probably find many opportunities to respond intelligently. Agreeing, disagreeing, and expanding upon what's been said by those with some influence is a terrific way to get noticed and be a part of the dialog.

A great way to expand on the dialog is to interview a knowledgeable blogger who has said something relevant to your space. Again, assuming that the solar energy market presents an opportunity for Acme Widgets, Acme might want to interview an expert who has blogged about the growth potential of solar energy, and may even probe the blogger to comment on why widgets might be relevant to this emerging power source. Recording and podcasting the interview can be an easy way to get the content up quickly, and you are almost certain to get an inbound link from the interviewee.

Reading, commenting, and blogging are the best ways to get the relevant bloggers to notice and link to you. Being a participant in the conversation and contributing valuable insights can reap rewards that far outweigh those of any calculated "outreach" campaign that the PR pros come up with.

Encouraging Comments and Trackbacks

Comments and trackbacks provide valuable feedback and input that can help you make your blog better. Lots of comments and discussion also provide a "community" aspect to your site that adds more value for your visitors. Think of these contributions to your site as "free content" that can further enhance your site's visibility.

We advise bloggers who allow their readers to contribute to the discussion via comments or trackbacks to do whatever they can to encourage those contributions. Provocative posts, asking for input, and other techniques are useful, but it's also important to incorporate an effective comment management system.

HOW SOLICITING AND LISTENING TO COMMENTS CAN SELL PRODUCTS

Mike Davidson used reader comments extensively to develop his popular Newsvine service that helps bloggers capture and post about current news events. As Mike was developing Newsvine, he used his personal blog to solicit ideas and feedback from his dedicated readers who were eager to participate in creating a new online service. He then invited a group of bloggers, colleagues, friends, and family to become a part of the beta testing program, and they ultimately defined how the final service worked. Thanks to the involvement of these readers and bloggers in the launch of a new product, he was able to generate early buzz that helped make it a success in the marketplace.

Similarly Shaun Inman developed the site statistics program Mint via his blog by posting prototype screen shots and asking for reader feedback. By listening closely to the comments that came in, he was able to better match his reader's needs, and found a ready and waiting market when he finally shipped the software.

This new breed of software developers is taking a new and open approach to creating and selling applications. Rather than keeping product plans secret and revealing them to a select few late in the game, they've learned that a blog-centric dialog during development can enhance the functionality and, ultimately, the sales of a new product.

You want to make commenting an easy, inviting, and rewarding process. Easy means no cumbersome registration forms. Inviting means not letting one commenter flame another. Rewarding means that comments are met with an affirmative response. On our blogs, we carefully moderate all comments that come in, and don't publish ones from readers that don't play nice with others. We also try as often as possible to respond directly to those who have taken the time to write us. Movable Type and WordPress allow blog authors to read and approve all comments before they go live. We discuss the different ways to deal with comments in Chapter 4.

Maintaining a Presence

While posting is the most important thing you can do to establish and maintain a presence in the blogosphere, there are many other options available that can help create or maintain a high profile for you and your business on the Web.

Commenting like crazy on posts that others write—especially on popular sites—not only reminds the big-time bloggers of your existence, but can also get other commenters to drop by and check out your blog.

Online discussions aren't just happening between bloggers. Discussion and community sites such as Yahoo! Groups and Google Groups provide good focused venues for raising awareness about your writing. Contribute to the dialog in these groups, and tactfully mention your blog at the same time.

Link out to other blogs. Most bloggers we know have created RSS feeds that inform them immediately when people link to their site. There is probably no better way to remind or "notify" influencers of your existence.

Go out there and talk to real, live people. Attending industry conferences are a great way to both spread the word and gather new information for your own posting efforts. Conferences today offer more and more opportunities to network, and as many tech bloggers will tell you, these gatherings provide a treasure trove of information and allow you to evangelize your efforts. Your blog is part of your business; treat it as such.

In general, get your blog's address out there as much as possible. Put the link in your signature that appears at the bottom of emails, and try to include it in all your marketing and collateral.

If you're passionate about your topic, diligent about seeking the bloggers where they live, enthusiastic and polite to others, and responsive to comments and feedback on your own site, then you can consider yourself to be engaged with the blogosphere. And the longer you remain firmly engaged, the more your readership will grow. In time—with work and luck—you'll see other bloggers using these same strategies to engage you in conversation.

Findability Rules

Findability is about making sure search engines see you and think you are relevant. The idea is that when your prospects type in searches, they see you at the top of the results list and the "other guys" fall below you.

Google is the Big Kahuna of search engines, and the methods they use to determine a site's importance are being emulated by the other search portals (Yahoo!, MSN, etc.). It's a safe bet that if Google "likes" you, the other search engines will too. With that in mind, here are some considerations to take into account as you get blogging.

Understanding How Google Sees You

If you ask a knowledgeable blogger where her visitors come from, she will likely tell you that a significant percentage of her clicks come from search referrals, and that Google is the one engine that outpaces all of the others. This was echoed in an April 2005 article in which Wired asserted that Google accounts for 4 out of 5 Web searches, and 75 percent of all referrals to Web sites.

With this in mind, bloggers need to understand how Google "sees" their sites, so they can focus some effort on ensuring that they stay on the good side of this critical traffic source. Don't get us wrong—we are not going to turn this into an "SEO" lecture. Search engine optimization has blossomed into a significant industry in the past few years, as organizations worldwide try to game the system and get their sites to come up higher in the rankings. Bloggers don't really need to understand all the intricacies of SEO. This is because much of the hard work has already been done for you by the blogging software, and normal blogging practices take care of much of the rest of it. With that in mind, here is a quick overview of the most important things Google looks at when it drops by your site for a visit.

- Who is linking in to you? Are there a lot of other reputable sites that link to your blog? Are they sites that Google feels are relevant and influential, or do they come from "link exchanges"?

■ How is your site built? Do you use clean HTML that adheres to known standards, or is it sloppy code that seems to work okay in a browser?

■ How frequently is your site updated? Does the site have significant new content since the last time Google visited, or is it unchanged?

Luckily for you, other bloggers will tend to link in if there is content of interest, and practically all blogging software writes HTML that Google respects. And all blogging engines use a CMS that makes content updates a snap.

Your server logs can also give you valuable information about how Google sees you. Most of the Web analysis programs in use today can tell you what search terms people used to find your site. Knowing what terms Google thinks fit your blog can help guide you with future posts.

Knowing Your Keywords

Because Google weighs your subject lines so heavily, it's a good idea to try and craft those title phrases to match what you believe your customers will be searching for, and to write subjects that align with popular search terms. When people type search phrases, Google will try to align these phrases with your titles—so be sure that the title of your post contains as many relevant search terms as possible. Beyond that, try to sprinkle the first 150 words of each post with the same key search terms.

But be careful. You may get a lot of visitors by posting about Britney Spears, but if projecting an image of "thought leadership" to a specific audience is your goal, you'll likely be barking up the wrong tree. A relatively even mix of relevant and popular phrases can help you achieve readership that is both large and interested.

But how can you determine what phrases are the most likely to drive a lot of relevant visitors your way? While your server logs and other traffic analysis systems can tell you what search phrases are bringing people to your site, they aren't telling you what other phrases your market is using.

One approach is to brainstorm what searches you think potential visitors might use. If you're blogging for the Maui tourism association, and getting lots of clicks from searches like "Maui condo rentals," you might want to consider broader phrases. Perhaps market research indicates that 28 percent of all Maui visitors are making their first trip to Hawaii, so "Hawaii vacation packages" could be a good phrase to target. The better you know your audience, the better you'll do at isolating terms that appeal to them.

There are several free online tools that can help you prioritize and expand on the search terms you feel make sense. Both Google and Yahoo! provide online utilities related to their advertising services (AdWords and Overture) that can help here. They can both be easily found by typing "Keyword Selector Tool" into either a Google or Yahoo! search.

If you type a search term into the Google AdWords Keyword Tool, it will respond with a broad set of "more specific" and "similar" keywords. For example, the word *Maui* suggested 131 other more specific phrases including *Maui beach vacation club*. In all, 172 similar terms were generated, including *Kauai*.

The Overture Keyword Selector Tool is not quite as good at making suggestions, but it's great at telling you how popular related searches are. When we entered *Maui* into the tool, it informed us that 96,343 Yahoo! searches were made in the previous month using that specific word. It also told us that *Maui Sheraton* was the most often searched for hotel, with 7,053 requests. One unexpected discovery was that the phrase *Maui wedding* outranked any and all hotels and condos, and was even more popular than golf-related searches. Knowing such information might allow you to shift your blog posting to better target newlyweds. Maybe a post titled "Maui Wedding Venues: North Coast Alternatives" would be a wise move.

Linking Matters

We already know that inbound links from other blogs and Web sites are critical for boosting your visibility with search engines, but what can be done to encourage those links?

Obviously, the more interesting your writing is, and the more you work to engage the blogosphere, the more people will link in. You should focus the majority of your efforts on these practices. That said, there are a few other tactics that can improve your chances of getting inbound links.

While most pro bloggers dislike receiving emails asking, "Hey, will you link to me?" a personal email simply notifying another blogger about a recent post that might be of interest can result in an inbound link.

One key to this strategy is to focus on quality, not quantity, of links. A few links from sites with high page rank is far better than a lot of links from sites with low page rank. If you are going to take the time to email others about your posts, focus on blogs that rank higher than your site does. You can download and install the Google Toolbar browser plug-in, which will tell you the PageRank of any site you visit. (PageRank is a Google feature and is discussed in Chapter 8, "Monitoring and Managing Your Blog.")

Getting listed in one of the various Web directories such as the Open Directory Project (*http://dmoz.org*) can also get you an inbound link that Google has deemed important. You can submit your blog to one of the categories they list, and if you're approved, you'll get a nice bit of Google juice.

TIP: Whatever you do, don't respond to any spam link exchange emails—the ones from strangers that say, "Link to me and I'll link back." Google is wise to that game, and may even penalize you if they sense you are partnering with a random, link-happy site.

There are some new services that, for a fee, will broker links from high-ranking sites that they have determined Google likely sees as related to your blog. We have heard that they can be effective. There are some risks with this approach, as Google strongly disapproves of the practice, and you have to avoid being taken by a dishonest service. We'd avoid taking any risks. We would encourage you to spend your cash on getting great writers instead.

One last bit of common-sense advice: Don't forget to be generous with your outbound links. Bloggers will often link back to you if they notice you are linking in.

Although the practice of search engine optimization is a subject that can fill volumes, crafting your site and your posts to align with your intended audience is the critical element. The resulting links can make your blog findable and will bring in many new readers. Remember that blogs are built to include SEO right from the get-go.

Posting Isn't Enough

Many prominent bloggers claim that the traditional channels for delivering corporate "messaging" are headed for the scrap heap thanks to the wonders of blogging. Naturally, many of these new media types are hailing blogs as the be-all, end-all for communicating with customers and potential customers.

While we agree that blogs, podcasts, and other new technologies are changing the world of traditional media, it's undeniable that leveraging older marketing tools can help bloggers broaden their audience, especially when they launch a blog. At this stage of the game, we feel the famous Monty Python line "I'm not dead yet" applies to many of these avenues.

We've paid close attention to how successful blogs have taken advantage of various "dying" forms of promotion. Here are a few inexpensive channels that we've seen yield rewards.

The Press Release Isn't Dead (Yet)

If you search for the phrase "the press release is dead," you'll find that this assertion has been made online by a variety of pundits since the dawn of the Web. In our early days of blogging, we even wrote posts saying the same thing.

But after doing a little more research—and issuing several of our own releases—we've discovered that while press releases don't provide as many home runs as they used to, they still get you on base.

Even if you're a diehard new media advocate, there are reasons press releases make sense. After testing the effectiveness of releases ourselves, we discovered that the more progressive newswire services are very effective at implanting your "news" into several highly visible RSS streams, and can greatly expand awareness in the blogosphere. This improves the odds of another blogger—or journalist—picking up on what you've written and writing about it themselves. In addition, press releases deliver a lot of inbound links. Thanks to the channels the newswires have available, releases get replicated all over the Web and any links in a release are seen by Google as positive linking activity. The bottom line is that a blog post tied to a release gets more attention than one that doesn't.

Many bloggers disdain press releases because the style they're written in is usually nauseating marketing-speak. We say: Don't confuse the channel with the content. You don't have to write that way. Many current releases are conversational and better reflect how people communicate today.

Advertising Online: Buying Readers

We've discovered firsthand that online advertising can be a great way to jump-start interest in a new blog or augment traffic to already established blogs. It's quite easy to get effective ads up and running, and campaigns can be designed to match any budget. Since it's an avenue few bloggers currently use to expand their readership, it can give you an edge in a world of increasing competition over eyeballs. Companies are also finding success by adding blogs to their long-running ads.

We buy text advertisements using mostly the Google AdWords system and Yahoo!'s Overture network. These ads appear on the search engines when people type in search terms that match phrases we've purchased, and also appear on Google and Yahoo! partner sites that fit the profile for these terms.

The easiest way to get started in the online advertising game is to sign up for a Google AdWords account. All you need is a charge card and the five minutes or so it takes to fill out the online forms. For the five-dollar setup fee, you'll be up and running. Go to Google and click the "Advertising Programs" link to get the process started. You'll be prompted through the steps required to get your first ad posted. Since you pay only when someone clicks on an ad, you don't need to worry about paying for ads that don't generate traffic.

We've also purchased—and traded for—graphical banner ad space on a variety of sites. That type of buy is a little more complex than buying search text ads, but can yield effective results. Like a roadside billboard, many banner placements will cost you money regardless of how many clicks you get, so we advise clients to begin with simple text ads to get a feel of how much traffic they want to achieve per dollar spent. Worry about buying banner space after you get some experience with search ads.

Working with the Press

Many of the biggest blogs have broken through and have received coverage in the mainstream media. One of the dirty little secrets of the blogosphere is that plenty of the stars of this "grassroots media" revolution have achieved their fame with the help of marketing firms that have worked hard to get them magazine, newspaper, and television coverage.

If you don't have a team of marketing and PR professionals at your disposal, how can you get this kind of visibility without breaking the bank? Other than sending out press releases, what can be done?

We've discovered that it's a good idea to connect with journalists that cover the same editorial space you do. The press is always on the lookout for good stories, and they appreciate anyone who can provide them with interesting leads. You might even already have connections with journalists who have covered your business in the past. Give them a call to offer a heads-up about your new blog. Because blogs are such a hot topic these days, you might even find that they want to write about your efforts. Targeting bloggers who also write for traditional publications can reap rewards. Creating entries that reinforce or refute points they've made in their blogs—and linking to them, of course—can get their attention.

Getting some friends with marketing resources to help you can also be a good strategy. Breaking a story that makes someone else look good can get them to assist in your publicity efforts. We've been able to create newsworthy posts in partnership with other organizations that have brought in their marketing teams to help spread the word. This has been the main method we've used to get mainstream coverage. One example was when we partnered with Connexion by Boeing to host a bunch of bloggers on a special flight to demonstrate their in-flight Internet service. That event led to a series of posts that brought coverage from the *Wall Street Journal* and NPR.

Issuing press releases, buying online ad space, and getting covered by the traditional press are promotional angles that 99 percent of the blogosphere is not pursuing. Those that do will have an edge, and we've seen it work firsthand with our own endeavors and those of our clients.

Getting noticed on the Web is a challenge, and requires hard work and smart execution. Although blogs provide an advantage over regular Web sites, we encourage you to use all of the tactics at your disposal to stand out.

Be interesting, strive for conversation, make Google a priority, and don't be afraid to use non-bloggy tools to help spread the word.

Chapter 8

Monitoring and Managing Your Blog

After you've launched your blog and have become accustomed to posting regularly, there are a variety of tasks that you'll want to add to your routine. The top bloggers and companies that publish blogs take time daily to leverage the many tools and services available to monitor their traffic, readership, and the discussion they generate.

This chapter will cover a few of the more important ways to monitor your blog's performance and will advise you on how you can stay on top of the conversation generated by your posts.

Watching Traffic

Relevant benchmarks and accurate measurement are the hallmarks of any properly executed business venture, and blogging is no exception. Legendary management gurus W. Edwards Deming and Peter Drucker wrote volumes on why and how to track the performance of business operations. Adherents to both Deming and Drucker agree, "what gets measured, gets done."

Fortunately, in this age of networked systems and powerful computers, we have an abundance of Web analytics tools that allow you to track the performance of your site. In many cases, these tools let you sneak a peek at how competitors are doing as well—and they're probably already installed on your server. If you don't have access, just ask your server administrators to add your blog to the stats program and get the results.

In 2006, longtime business blogger Darren Rowse (*www.problogger.net*) asked his readers what statistics they wanted most from their analytics reports. Several dozen bloggers responded. Their four main categories—in order of importance—were:

- How are people finding my blog?

- How large is my audience, and is it growing?

- What do my visitors like/dislike about my blog?

- How much money am I making from advertising?

In this section, we'll cover what types of measurements are available to help answer these questions, and what tools and services you can use to measure your—and others'—sites.

Tools

While most blog services and engines come with built-in tools for analyzing traffic and visitor activity, they tend to lack the depth and detailed reporting capabilities that most professional bloggers and companies need. It's almost certain that any serious blogger will need to incorporate some kind of external tracking service or system if they want properly detailed visitor activity reports. These reports aren't only for geeks who like to delve into the minutiae of site activity. They are extremely useful for writers who want to see how their posts and campaigns are resonating with readers, and for managers to report statistics on blog activity to their bosses.

To be specific, most site managers and bloggers want reports that provide:

- **Referral information:** What link did someone click to get to my blog? Who is sending me traffic?

- **Unique visitors:** How many different people come to my blog in a given period?

- **Page views:** How many pages/posts on my blog do people look at when they are visiting? Which ones?

- **Search terms:** What search phrases do people use to find my blog?

FORGET ABOUT HITS

Experienced bloggers don't really care much about "hits." Hits are not nearly as useful as page views or unique visitors when describing site traffic. Hits indicate how many single elements on a page a viewer downloads. Each image on your page counts as a hit, so a single visitor can easily log dozens of hits in a single visit. Also, each page or post can have different numbers of elements. Measuring blog traffic by counting hits is sort of like describing how long a plane ride is by counting clouds. A much better measure to focus your attention on is unique visitors.

There are literally dozens of software programs and services that can capture and analyze blog data, so choosing the best one can be extremely challenging. Most will readily provide the information listed above, so you can survive nicely without having the "perfect" one in place. In addition, you can add new analysis services at any time, and they usually won't conflict with those already in use.

Even though you can easily win at the metrics game, it's good to know how these programs work, and to understand a few of the key differences between them. That way you can get a suitable one up and running quickly and can take advantage of the power available without delay.

There are two different technological approaches to blog analysis, and both have their own unique advantages and disadvantages. If you are subscribing to a hosted service (such as TypePad, Blogger, or BlogHarbor), you can easily install a bit of JavaScript code on your pages that will send traffic information to a tracking service hosted elsewhere on the Web. You can then go to that service's Web site to view your stats. Most individual bloggers use this approach.

If you have access to the server that is hosting your blog—if, for example, your blog is tied in with your company's Web site—you have the additional option of installing software that analyzes your server log files. Server logs record just about every interaction that visitors have with your site, and various programs can manipulate the unfiltered log information and generate useful reports. If you host your own blog, you no doubt have analysis software already installed and available. We suggest that you ask your Webmaster for access to these reports.

These server log analysis programs (such as Analog, Webalizer, AWStats, Urchin, NetTracker, WebTrends, and ClickTracks) will crunch the data your server creates and publish reports that provide answers to the questions above. The advantage to using these programs is that they don't impose any overhead on visitors' browsers, and they capture a lot of information. The downside is that bloggers may not have access to the stats program, and some complain that the reports include too much data (such as visits by robots and search engines) that aren't truly visitor-related.

JavaScript-based services include Google Analytics, StatCounter, Site Meter, AddFreeStats, OneStat, and many more. After you create an account with these services, they provide you with some code designed to be implanted on your pages. Soon after that's done, you can log in and see reports that show the activity on your site. The advantages here are that you get visitor-focused reports, and that almost any blogger can install and use these services. The problem is that the JavaScript imposes a load on your pages, and if the analysis service is having technical problems, it can conceivably prevent your pages from loading as they should. Also, a small percentage of users will have JavaScript turned off and their activities will not be recorded.

TIP: Measure Map (*www.measuremap.com*) and Mint provide analysis services that are considered to be some of the best in terms of visual layout and appearance. Design professionals love the way these programs serve up their visitor reports. If you are a visual person who demands information presented in an aesthetic style that makes numbers easy to digest, we recommend that you investigate these two options.

Based on our own experience and what we hear from other top bloggers, our advice is to start by reviewing the reports that your server generates (if you have access to those servers), and install StatCounter or Google Analytics (both free) tracking code on your pages. Google Analytics is ideal for those bloggers using Google's AdWords or AdSense because you can track ad revenues and performance. But it's not for the total newbie or those who get overwhelmed by screenfuls of charts and graphs. For those who just want the facts, StatCounter is a great way to go. Most managers will discover that either of these services will make it easy for them to get most of the information they need.

Feed Readership

While site traffic is readily measured and analyzed, measuring feed readership is a different story. As we mentioned in Chapter 4, "Designing for Readers," you can use a service called FeedBurner, which issues feeds for you, and provide reports that are far more detailed than what any blogging tool currently provides. FeedBurner reports include information on how many subscribers you have, what types of newsreaders your subscribers use, and readership over time.

Some bloggers hesitate to use the service because they fear that they'll be "locked in" and won't be able to go back to issuing their regular feeds without losing their current FeedBurner subscribers. Fortunately, the FeedBurner folks have set up a forwarding service that can help most of your subscribers easily realign to your original feeds should you decide to disengage from FeedBurner.

Comparing Traffic

Financial managers spend much of their time correlating the numbers their accountants provide with industry and competitive benchmarks. For many high-level executives, the ability to meet or beat certain competitive ratios is directly linked to their compensation. In most serious industries and professions, it's vital to know what your partners and competitors are achieving.

The competitive landscape is no different in the blogosphere. It's great to know how your site is doing in terms of visibility and traffic, but it's even better to understand how you compare to others—especially blogs hosted by competitors. This kind of analysis is tricky. While public companies openly provide many of their key financial indicators, very few organizations provide their server log files for analysis.

Fortunately, there are several tools available that can provide a peek into your competitor's numbers and give you a good idea of how you stack up to other Web sites and blogs.

Alexa

One of the most widely used site comparison tools is Alexa (*www.alexa.com*). Several million Web surfers—Alexa does not disclose the exact figure—have installed the Alexa Toolbar within their Web browsers. These enhanced browsers track all sites the user visits. That data is then sent back to Alexa, which generates reports that visitors can access for free.

A primary measurement that Alexa provides is a site's traffic "rank," which indicates where a site places compared to the rest of the Web (top 10, top 100, top 1000, etc.). If you visit Alexa.com, you can enter up to five URLs into its Traffic History Graph and see where those sites placed daily for up to a year of activity.

Alexa is an imperfect tool. It only tracks surfers using Windows and Internet Explorer, so information from Apple and Linux computers is never compiled. Also, people who surf with Firefox and other browsers are ignored. There are some who complain that this makes the service irrelevant. We disagree. Our belief is that since it likely skews the results from competitive sites in a similar direction, it's still a relevant way to compare two sites that share similar attributes. Even a defective yardstick can tell you if one object is longer than another.

SiteMeter

One tool bloggers use to measure their own traffic statistics is SiteMeter. With this software, you have the option of making your statistics public, which can provide a handy reference for potential advertisers. With public stats, those who want to buy space on your site can quickly see how popular your blog really is.

There is also a chance that a competitor or other site of interest may have made their stats public, so it might be worth a look. A site called The Truth Laid Bear (*http://truthlaidbear.com/*) compiles public SiteMeter data for several hundred sites, so you can scan for blogs that might align with your needs.

Inbound Links

PageRank is an indicator Google uses to describe how relevant your site is, largely based on inbound links. It uses a scale from 1 to 10 (1 being least relevant, 10 being most). The Google toolbar utility will tell you the PageRank of any site you visit, and it is easily installed in most browsers. There are also several Web sites that allow you to enter a URL to test a site's PageRank. PageRank is not really an indicator of traffic, but it is one more way to see how you compare to other blogs in terms of Google relevance.

While PageRank approximates inbound links, you can get a more precise count by using Google to do an inbound link search. Also, if you head to Technorati.com, you can enter a site's URL and it will tell you how many blogs link to it. You can even use this service to track the number of inbound links to a specific post. Bloggers frequently refer to the number of inbound links as measured by Technorati as a preferred indicator.

 TIP: To search for inbound links on Google, type in *link:http://www.yourwebsitehere.com/*.

More than Numbers

Some bloggers we know confess that they are addicted to watching their stats, and spend hours poring over their referrer logs, monitoring the source of every inbound click.

While numbers are important, don't let them be the main focus of your efforts. The most respected companies host blogs because they feel a need to express themselves and have something interesting to say to their customers. They also realize that it's hard to influence traffic with any individual post, and instead take a more long-term approach.

Post frequently, write insightfully, and check your traffic periodically to see who is listening. Focus on the writing and the rest should fall into place.

Discovering Trends

Engaged bloggers monitor more than dry statistics about clicks and page views. Much of the most interesting and relevant information about the blogosphere relates to the conversational side of the space.

Find out who is talking about you and what they're saying. Also, pay attention to the bloggers who talk about other blogs of interest to those in your competitive space. Staying on top of those conversations can help you write more interesting and relevant posts.

Bring the Buzz

Chances are that you don't have time to keep your finger constantly on the pulse of the blogosphere, or even your little corner of it. But for all of the reasons we've talked about, it's important to understand what's going on in the world beyond your blog. That's why there are a number of tools that, when properly used, can give you good information without a huge investment of time.

Technorati

When you ask a blogger what site they default to when they want a quick check on who is linking to them, more often than not they'll say that Technorati is the place they go.

We've mentioned Technorati before: it's a blog search engine that monitors millions of sites and over a billion links with the intent to provide a real-time analysis of who is saying what, and who is referring to whom. Almost every report and search they provide can be saved as a "watchlist" with a related RSS feed so that you can view this information in your newsreader.

Beyond their core service of showing current linking and posting activity, they also offer data about what bloggers have the most authority, and categorize posts and blogs into topical groupings that make following industry buzz even easier.

Due to their popularity and the exploding growth of the blogosphere, Technorati has struggled with intermittent outages and slowdowns that have frustrated many of their dedicated users. They also have a problem with randomness in their reports. As Mark Twain said, "Facts are stubborn, but statistics are more pliable." Be sure to understand that all the stats programs and search engines are not an exact science or perfect.

BlogPulse

Intelliseek is a company that has been tracking Internet discussions and commentary for many years. They were one of the first organizations to attempt the gathering of online "word-of-mouth" information with the goal of creating reports for marketers and other researchers.

When blogging emerged as a source of significant online conversation, Intelliseek created several buzz tracking tools specifically built for monitoring the blogosphere. These BlogPulse tools graphically show how much discussion is going on about any blog, topic, or blog post, and are updated constantly.

Corporate subscribers to Intelliseek services pay a lot of money for access to the full suite of reporting tools, but an impressive set of useful reports can be had for free at *www.blogpulse.com.* Some of the more useful reports include:

Trend Search is shown in **Figure 8.1**. Trend searches will graphically depict buzz about any search term you enter. In the fall of 2005, the editors of Harvard Business School's *Working Knowledge Newsletter* cited Trend Search as one of their favorite BlogPulse offerings. We agree with their assessment that "this information will not only give you links to specific content about your product generated around the Web, but also provide a view into what specifically generates interest in your product or company."

Imagine that you have launched a new product and want to see if there is any surge in related discussion, or perhaps a competitor has a new offering and you want to see the impact. Trend Search can show you the conversational activity as it happens.

Figure 8.1

Note the huge spike in iPod mentions on December 26, 2005. Clicking through reveals many bloggers discussing what Santa put under the tree for them.

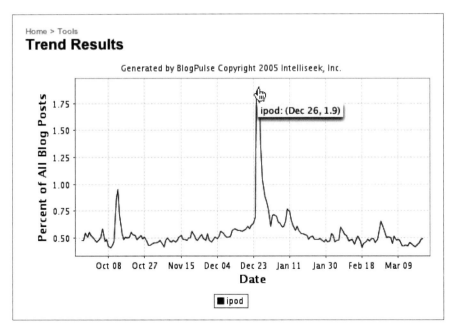

Conversation Tracker allows users to follow a threaded view of conversations based on any posts you (or others) make. This is handy for seeing both the quantity and evolution of discussion on any topic.

BlogPulse's Profiles provide details about specific blogs and blog authors. They are useful for gathering intelligence about the blogging activity of partners and competitors. Posting behavior, linking activity, influence measures, and author information is captured and updated.

Google

Google is best known for indexing the Web and providing search services for all kinds of content. But it has a lesser-known search capability that focuses exclusively on blog sites. As with other blog-only search portals, Google Blog Search provides RSS feeds of any blog search you make (there are still no RSS feeds available for regular Google searches, however), so you can be updated via newsreader as new mentions appear.

Google Blog Search offers some advantages over other tools that can be useful when you are in buzz-tracking mode. One advantage is that the enormous computing horsepower Google puts behind its search tools makes it the fastest at presenting results. Another is that it can apply its relevancy PageRank to the results it finds. All of the other engines present their matches sorted by date—and so can Google—but sorting by relevance provides a way to easily see what bloggers with a higher degree of influence are saying.

Google also has an advanced search option that allows you to search blogs by author, date, and URL. This means that you can get feeds from specific blogs filtered by keywords. It's one way to get more focused results and avoid having to subscribe to all the posts a blogger makes. All you have to do is enter some keywords and the URL of a blog that you want to track, and Google will create a feed that looks for just those specific matches.

Buzz, Memes, and Blogospheria

Most blog posts live a quiet life and take on a fairly dormant existence. They go up, a few clicks come in, maybe some inbound links are established, and then they sit there patiently waiting for someone new to drop by and read them. Occasionally, though, a post catches on in a big way. It resonates strongly with visitors, and the result is a lot of comments, links, and traffic.

In rare cases, a post or a portion of a post will become a *meme* and replicate wildly, taking on a life of its own.

Memes include catch phrases like "Snakes on a Plane"—inspired by the Samuel L. Jackson film with its amusingly straightforward title—and the enduring "Wazzzzup" (originating from a Budweiser ad), both of which almost instantly hurtled from obscurity to becoming universally understood parts of online discussion. In blogging circles, the word *meme* has started to mean more or less a nugget of information that is being discussed widely. A discrete piece of information with a lot of buzz is often referred to as being *meme-worthy*.

TIP: To learn more about memes, see the extensive Wikipedia article on the topic at *http://en.wikipedia.org/wiki/Meme.*

The ongoing chatter created by bloggers discussing posts, news, and other happenings is often referred to as the *blogospheria*, and it's where memes will take root.

While many memes are created unintentionally, it's possible to craft a saying, post, or site that purposefully spreads like wildfire. JibJab's political cartoons and Burger King's subservient chicken site—where you can type in commands that a man in a chicken suit will obey—are examples of successful meme-making in recent years. We built traffic on Pugblog partly by creating a small meme. We parodied podcasting by creating "pugcasts" that featured Cap'n barking to a backbeat. These audio broadcasts caught on, got blogged, and eventually made it into the iTunes podcast directory. While not a major online phenomenon, the traffic has been substantial.

Sometimes meme-making campaigns can work against you, as Dr. Pepper/7Up learned with their ill-fated Raging Cow blog. Their marketing agency's effort to promote a new flavored milk product by quietly ingratiating themselves with selected bloggers backfired, and resulted in a negative reaction from the blogosphere.

If one of your posts catches on, the resulting buzz can be detected and monitored using a variety of online services that measure both positive and negative trends. Naturally, it's good to be on top of the latest memes, and to also be aware if one of your posts is catching fire in this way.

Memetrackers

With meme-tracking becoming more and more important to trend-watching bloggers, specialized sites have emerged that automate the process of finding what's hot and ignoring what's not. Three of the most popular sites that specialize in compiling what's buzzing in the blogosphere are Digg (*www.digg.com*), Memeorandum (*www.memeorandum.com*), and Tailrank (*www.tailrank.com*).

Other relevant sources of blogospheria include Technorati's Popular page (*www.technorati.com/pop/*) and Daypop's Top 40 links (*www.daypop.com/top/*), where the up-to-the-minute chatter is logged.

These sites closely monitor which posts are being referenced frequently by influential bloggers, and then compile, sort, and present them for review. It's possible to search within these compiled topics and save your search results as an RSS feed.

Tailrank even allows you to import the entire set of feeds you currently subscribe to, so it can apply its ranking algorithms to your favorite blogs. That way it can identify the most promising subjects that relate to your areas of interest.

Comments and Interactions

Because blogging is a medium that invites interaction and so many businesses are using blogs to promote their products and companies, they can become an attractive venue for all kinds of discussion and debate.

Expert bloggers employ a variety of techniques to help keep the dialog on track and to serve their visitors as well as their business interests.

Defining the Conversation

While fostering conversation is one compelling reason to begin a blog, it should be recognized that bloggers have the ability to define the discussion and steer the dialog—at least on their own sites. Beyond that, it can be argued that they have a responsibility to their readers to make sure contributions by others add value and insight to the online conversation.

Not everyone agrees with the idea of moderation and filtering of comments. Some feel that the "censoring" of discussion is against the spirit of the blogosphere. While we commend their idealism, we find that unmoderated discussion is generally not a practical strategy for a business-oriented blog. For one thing, we doubt that a business of any consequence would get into blogging knowing that the blog could likely become a bulletin board for unfiltered dissent and criticism. We've been in far too many meetings with corporate representatives to even suggest that a totally open, uninhibited, free-for-all is the way to go. It's clear that an idea like that is simply a nonstarter.

One way to think of your blog is as a virtual conference room in which you're hosting an open meeting. In that setting, a certain amount of civility, relevance, intelligence, and decorum is expected. Guests who stand up and pontificate on a subject should show respect for the other people present.

This is why we like having a system in which all comments are previewed before they go live. On our blog, many comments go up and a few don't. We think that if people want to write graffiti, they should find a different setting than our conference room. If your blog system doesn't allow preapproval, a far-distant second choice is to delete unwanted comments when they appear.

Posting a comment policy so that it's available to readers can help you define the conversation, and can prevent inappropriate contributions in the first place. A simple Google search for "blog comment policy" will help you with ideas to create your own. You can read our policy on all of our blogs. Some of the common threads that run through these policies include the mandates that comments must be on-topic, they must not contain personal attacks or insults, and cannot include profanity. In many cases, no anonymous commenters are allowed.

Most of our clients and partners are primarily concerned with how to deal with critical comments. But when you keep in mind that even Mother Teresa had her detractors, it's hard to believe that a blog representing a for-profit venture won't receive some negativity from a few readers. With that in mind, the question is what do you do when you get comments that are far from complimentary?

First of all, we don't believe that criticism is necessarily a bad thing, to be avoided at all costs. Since blogs put a human face on a company, when a savvy blogger takes on a critic, it diffuses the negativity that could have been focused and amplified in a different venue. It's a bit like a lightning rod. Compared to other structures, a building with a lightning rod does stand a greater chance of taking a strike. But it also deflects and diffuses a bolt that could have been devastating elsewhere.

Constructive criticism is easy to deal with—remember how quickly Boeing improved their blog in response to negative comments. Things like "I find your manuals hard to read, because the print is too small" merit a thank you, and may require further investigation and could result in beneficial changes. Random insults that don't contribute are also easy to deal with. "Megacorp sucks!" is an example of something that would never go up on the site.

Dealing with critical comments that may highlight an embarrassing and/or accurate representation of a company's shortcomings takes a little more effort and finesse. You can often win at this game by responding with an honest, frank assessment of the situation as you see it. Most employee bloggers are to some degree insulated from the brunt of corporate criticism because they are not the corporate entity itself. Emphasizing the long hours you and your teammates put in toward the goal of creating quality products can help steer the conversation to the good things the company is doing.

A calm, polite, and noncombative stance is essential to taking control of the conversation. It minimizes the chances that you'll end up in a protracted debate, and taking the high road enhances the odds that another reader will step in and come to your defense by commenting on your behalf.

What if you are facing criticism that comes from posts on other blogs? While you certainly have less control on a blog that's not yours, you still may want to either comment there, or perhaps post and link to the criticism with your response. The same calm, honest approach that emphasizes your personal side to the story can steer things in a more positive direction. It's generally a good idea to see if any other bloggers link into it, or if comments start appearing before stepping in. There is a chance that the critical post may not be noticed or propagated.

Knowing When to Let Go

While staying on top of the conversation is an essential part of blogging, and stonewalling is impractical, one of the nice things you'll discover is that many issues are self-resolving. If you have an active and supportive community of readers, they will often step up to the plate and say what you think needs to be said. For that reason, we think you'll at times want to hold back a bit and see what develops before jumping into the fray.

In early 2005, we were visible partners with a corporate client on a fairly significant promotion intended to raise their awareness in the blogosphere. We knew that bloggers were touchy about this kind of thing, so we worked very hard to make sure it was an initiative that added something worthwhile to the discussion. When it launched, we sat hunched over our monitors for several days carefully monitoring Technorati and the other blog-monitoring sites to see what was being said in response. The resulting commentary was overwhelmingly positive, but eventually one negative post appeared that we hoped wouldn't propagate. We responded immediately with comments that gently refuted the negative position. Instead of solving the problem, it sent a signal that we were nervous and concerned, which was picked up on. Fortunately, none of this went anywhere, but we learned the lesson that timing is everything.

In that case, it would have been a better idea to wait and see if the negativity was reinforced or refuted by another comment or post. If nothing was said, we likely would have had no need to step in. If someone had stepped up to defend the project, we would not have needed to support our initiative. If someone had intelligently reinforced the criticism on the blog, that likely should have provided the trigger for action.

Waiting also lets you craft a response that is more thoughtful, better argued, and less emotional. No doubt there have been occasions when you've wisely decided to hold off for 24 hours before hitting the send button on an email. That same strategy is useful when it comes to publishing posts or comments in response to something another blogger has said.

Now that you've learned how to monitor what the blogosphere is talking about, who's visiting your blog, and commenting about your posts, we'll talk about where this whole blogging thing is headed in Chapter 9, "Beyond Blogging."

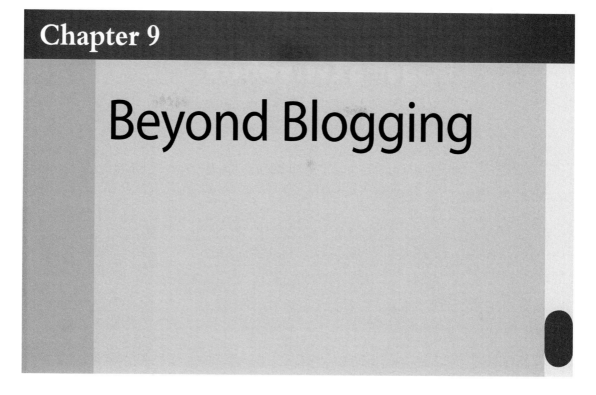

Chapter 9

Beyond Blogging

There's a joke that Steve likes to tell when he introduces himself to people as a business blogger. "Hi," he says, "I'm from the future."

Funny as it may sound, it's the truth. For many businesses and publishers, blogging *is* the future. And by that, we don't just mean the public relations or marketing blog—we mean all the various technologies that have been developed to help blogs get situated, published, and user-friendly. When you think about it, what we've been talking about in this book goes beyond blogging. We've been involved with the Web for years, and we haven't seen so many exciting new developments since its emergence way back in the '90s.

This chapter is about where we—and a lot of other talented people— see all of this going. We predict that the Web will continue to grow as a collaborative space, bringing businesses and customers closer.

Blogging Everywhere

If you've come this far, chances are that you've become enthusiastic about blogging and what it can do for your business. You should be excited about what you can accomplish, and how easy it is to get started. If so, you're not alone. Every day, thousands of businesses launch blogs and begin to reap the benefits of the blogosphere.

As the number of blogs and bloggers increases, you can bet that business blogs are going to become more and more ubiquitous. You could even say that they—and the capabilities that make them so powerful—will be everywhere in the coming years. What's more, the blogging technologies that we've talked about in this book will be increasingly applied to conventional Web sites. Blogs won't just be everywhere in their current form, they'll become a part of the architecture behind every Web site you see.

Syndicate or Die

Syndication technology really took hold with blogs, but indications are that all sites, blog or not, will be hopping on the syndication bandwagon. Considering that all the latest Web browsers and next-generation operating systems are enthusiastically supporting the technologies that drive syndication (RSS and Atom), it's clear that providing feeds will give all Web sites a significant advantage.

Among blog-savvy people, there is a growing sense of a fatigue with non-syndicating sites. Why take the time to hunt for new and relevant information when it can be delivered straight to you as it appears? As people grow accustomed to being notified when new content is available, sites that still don't syndicate may see a catastrophic drop in readership. Eventually, stand-alone brochureware sites could vanish altogether.

Considering that there are a number of services dedicated to creating RSS feeds from sites that have none (as we discussed in Chapter 7, "Launching Your Blog and Getting Noticed"), even non-blogs can—and should—be syndicating their content. Most newspapers have caught onto this, and their sites typically offer RSS feeds of their headlines at the very least.

You can expect to see syndication becoming a standard feature on most Web sites, and bloggers will continue to lead the way in driving the adoption of this critical delivery platform.

USERS WANT RSS

A good example of how central RSS is becoming to the success of any site is the story of TDF Blog (*www.tdfblog.com*) , which focuses on the Tour de France.

When it launched, TDF Blog was the only bike-racing site on the Web that offered RSS. Its competitors were all traditional Web sites that offered interesting content, but no way to notify readers of updates. In July 2005, TDF blog received 800,000 page views, while its competitors saw traffic drop.

In order to keep up with the blogs, even traditional Web sites will need to grow RSS feeds. Users have become accustomed to syndication, and may not want to be bothered with following a site that doesn't offer it, blog or not.

Is That a Blog?

Blogging tools are getting more sophisticated every day, and as the capabilities they offer start to rival expensive content management systems, blog sites will look less like personal diary sites. What we will see is complex and intricate Web sites with professionally designed layouts driven by blog software.

MSNBC's Rising from Ruin blog (*http://risingfromruin.msnbc.com*) doesn't look like a typical blog site. That's part of what makes it such a compelling portrait of post-Katrina Mississippi. You don't automatically identify it as a diary, so you look at the content without any preconceived notions of what you'll find.

Despite its unbloggy appearance (shown in **Figure 9.1**), Rising from Ruin has all the features that make a blog different from a traditional Web site. There's an RSS feed. There are archives and comments. The blog even has categories, but each facet is organized in a more flexible and organic layout.

In the future, many blogs will look and even behave much as ordinary Web sites do now. There will be as many different ways to organize content as there are bloggers to generate it. The key differences will all lie beneath the surface, making blogs infinitely more powerful than traditional Web sites, while retaining their aesthetic appeal.

Figure 9.1

MSNBC's blog covering post-Katrina Mississippi has all the features of a blog, but doesn't look like one.

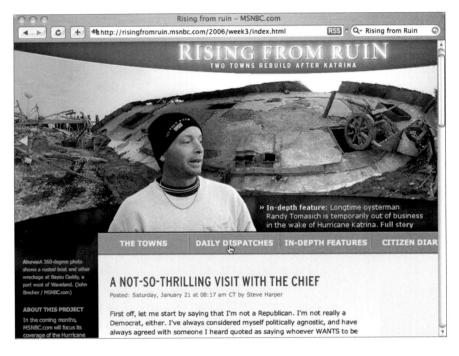

Internal Blogs and Wikis

The most talked-about business blogs are those that are available for public consumption. These "external" blogs are important. But "internal" blogs, designed to foster communication within and between teams, are becoming more prevalent. Internal blogs are only viewable to those who are directly involved and authorized. They use traditional blogging software and formats to create a powerful collaboration tool.

Internal communication via the Web is a tricky thing. Properly managed, online workflows can be incredibly productive and satisfying. But often, teams become ensnared in a mess of emails and attachments that can slow down even the most well-planned and organized project.

Used properly, internal blogs can free you from that frustrating morass. Their inherent organizational properties make it easy to categorize and cross-categorize posts and hold discussions among teammates scattered across the country or around the world. One of the perks of this system is that if someone new joins the team, they can bring themselves up to speed with relatively little difficulty just by reading the archives. As blogging continues to catch on, more companies will begin to use team blogs—well-secured from the outside world, of course—to organize and communicate about projects.

Another collaborative Web tool that many bloggers use is a *wiki*. The underlying technology that creates blogs and wikis is similar, so they are somewhat related. A wiki is a Web site that multiple authors can control. Imagine a bunch of chefs working on a casserole. One is in charge of tomatoes, one the meat, and another the cheese. After putting all the ingredients in and before it's baked, a chef can jump in and add more spices, remove some cheese, or do whatever she feels will make the best casserole, even if it's not her recipe. In other words, everyone has access to the file, and can change it to reflect their input. One of the many ways businesses use wikis is when developing complex documents.

Many bloggers use Basecamp, a wiki-like, blog-based tool from 37 Signals, to manage project communication and related files. Basecamp (*www.basecamphq.com*) is essentially a private group blog with posts, comments, and file management. It's a simple and easy-to-use system that keeps email traffic down and allows teams to upload documents, post ideas, and discuss the project. And just as with a blog, team members can receive updates via RSS feeds.

While the public blogosphere will continue to grow as a space for both businesses and consumers, we expect that this private blogosphere will grow even faster. Even businesses that decide to forgo a public blog will find that private, internal blogs and wikis are key to helping them communicate internally, complete projects, and accomplish goals more efficiently.

Blogging Anywhere

The rapid pace of technological change means that the tools used to interact with the Web—especially while on the go—have become more sophisticated. This trend will obviously continue, and as it does, more and more users will be accessing and creating Web content from devices other than traditional Web browsers. Businesses will need to remain cognizant of these changes if they want to keep up with the increasing demands of their customer bases.

Content on Demand

If you've ever received an email on your cell phone or viewed a Web site from your PDA, you've already experienced *divergence*. Some call the ability for multiple devices to work with content *convergence*, but divergence may be a more accurate term because it means that content is being experienced in numerous formats.

Web experts who promote standards-based technologies have been warning for years that content would be viewed and created on many different devices, and that day is upon us. We predict that the trend will continue, giving people endless options about how and where they want to experience content, and how they will share it with the world.

People are becoming accustomed to getting content that they can use on whatever device suits them. This is why services like the iTunes Music Store are making money hand over fist. More and more consumers want their music and videos to be available via computers, television, portable devices, or whatever platform fits the moment. For example, the popular social networking site MySpace recently became available via two new cellular phone models from Helio. This offers a lesson for business owners. If you offer content of any kind, more and more people are going to want to view it in whatever format is most convenient for them. If you don't offer that flexibility, they may go to your competitors.

Purina has been a leader in providing content in several formats and to many devices. They've figured out how to extend their brand by offering animal advice podcasts, ringtones and wallpapers for users' cell phones, and text message–powered pet tips. They've found multiple ways to reach pet owners by providing them with compelling content that builds trust and reinforces brand loyalty. If this content were only available via their Web site, you can bet that they would reach only a fraction of their current audience.

SOCIAL NETWORKS

At present, social networks like MySpace and Facebook are just what they sound like: sites where people—mostly students and young professionals—can link up with friends, share photos, and stalk former significant others. In fact, it seems pretty silly at first glance.

But there are a couple of reasons why social networking should matter to businesspeople. The first is that early adopters of social networking platforms also tend to be early adopters of other technologies. Staying aware of the trends in social networking will help you keep track of what else is new on the Web, as well as the behaviors and interests of an important demographic. And when you understand how these sites work, and what features they offer, you'll be better equipped to offer content that your readers will appreciate.

There's also a broader, more human reason why these sites have such long-term potential. Social networking appeals to people for the same reasons that blogging does: We all want to be seen and heard, and we all seek approval from society. Social networks allow users to piece together a profile that represents their "coolest self" from a milieu of multimedia elements. This concept is so compelling that MySpace—the most popular of the social networking sites at the time of this writing—recently surpassed MSN in traffic and is on pace to surpass Yahoo! as the number one site on the Web in the next few months.

As the sites that offer social networking continue to improve and expand, this mode of communication will become as ubiquitous as email. In time, it may well be integrated with most of the functions of the Web and will be an important way for businesses to understand Web trends and reach their customer bases.

Moblogging

Divergence means that in addition to downloading and experiencing content anywhere, people will create it and distribute it from anywhere. Bloggers are doing this today by *moblogging*, or mobile blogging.

With moblogging, many different types of media (audio, video, images, and text) can be instantly posted to a blog via the cellular phone network using phones and other portable devices. This means bloggers can create timely content without needing access to a personal computer or a standard Web connection.

There are a variety of mobile technologies that make all of this a snap. One example is AudioBlog (*www.audioblog.com*), a service that allows users to record and post podcasts directly from their mobile phones. The company was founded by expert blogger and podcaster Eric Rice. In November 2005, AudioBlog licensed a similar service to a Japanese company called Castella (*www.castella.jp*).

"The United States is a PC-based society," Rice told us, "while Japan is much more mobile-phone oriented. They really fly on those phones over there, so we knew that being able to podcast instantly from anywhere would translate well."

In various parts of the world, particularly Japan, businesses are using moblogging technology to send photos and data from the field to key managers in other locations. While we were writing this book, moblogging pioneer Mie Yaginuma (*www.kokochi.com*) told us that "in Japan, businesses moblog their factories, products being developed, and customers using those products. In the future, we expect companies all over the world to moblog from the floor of an expo or trade show and use their moblog entries as visual trip reports."

With cell phones being the primary mode of communication throughout much of the developing world, it's likely that this technology will make the Web and blogs in particular more accessible to a large and untapped audience.

Audio and Video

Fewer and fewer of your customers and prospects connect to the Web using a dial-up modem connection these days. With the prevalence of broadband connectivity, it's getting to be a safe bet that most visitors to your blog can easily access video and audio content online.

In the last few years, we've seen a surge in the number of bloggers who provide large media files on their sites. This will increase greatly over the coming years as the tools used to record, edit, and post these files become less expensive and easier to use.

Apple and other companies have created products specifically intended to help bloggers record, film, edit, and upload podcasts and videocasts with ease. It's simple for authors to include their video and audio creations in the iTunes Store's massive library of podcasts, which means that it will become infinitely easier for content creators to broaden their audiences.

It's clear that this trend toward rich media will continue, and we encourage all business bloggers to work on incorporating some video and/or audio in their posts.

Sales on the Go

In Chapter 4, "Designing for Readers," we talked about the customer who bought a Clip-n-Seal from the deck of a ferry by using his PDA. These sorts of sales are just the tip of the iceberg. As pay-by-cell-phone services such as TextPayMe grow more mainstream, more goods and services will be available via mobile payment systems.

Just as businesses should be aware that users will want content on demand, they should also expect that users will want flexibility in how they pay for content, goods, and services. Businesses must therefore be careful to ensure that people can pay them using the same devices they use to experience content.

As the Web becomes more accessible and collaborative, businesses will need to find ways to communicate with their customers using avenues that transcend the traditional tools used for online communication.

In this new world, the businesses that understand and respond to their customers with varied content provided via multiple sources will find the largest audience.

Small Teams, Big Things

One of the key features of a blog that we've outlined in this book is the flexibility that they offer. That flexibility, combined with the versatility offered by standards-based design, will give an edge to businesses that make the best use of these new technologies.

As we've said many times, blogs allow you to get information out there quickly. From planning to launch, a blog is extremely easy to create and simple to update. As more organizations realize this, we'll see specialized, focused blogs designed to deal with narrow topics or issues such as crisis management. Businesses will also learn—as Boeing did with Randy's Journal—that the blogosphere affords them a kind of online nimbleness that they've never seen before. Since blogs aren't monolithic Web sites that are updated every two years, we'll see more real-time product development and smaller, faster, quicker revision cycles to goods and services.

THE WATCHDOG

In early spring 2006, a four-month-old puppy was tragically burned to death with acid in Washington State. King County Animal Control cremated the animal's remains before the necessary investigation could take place; the crime is still unsolved. Within days, an animal-rights group called Pasado's Safe Haven had set up a blog that monitored law enforcement's handling of the case (*http://pasado.typepad.com/the_watchdog/*). A few days later, the blog had more than 100 comments from people voicing their outrage, and many commenters turned up at a town meeting with police. The blog has helped Pasado's galvanize their following and provide their audience with updates and information about the case.

We'll also see more creative—and sometimes ephemeral—uses of blogging, especially blogs that target young audiences and cover emerging trends. Businesses will clamor to sponsor and start blogs that focus on issues of interest to today's young people—from college admissions to extreme sports. We will almost certainly see an uptick in the number of blogs and podcasts started by celebrities designed to promote their latest films, CDs, or tours— as actor/musician Jack Black did for *Nacho Libre* (*www.nacholibre.com*) and director Peter Jackson did for *King Kong* (*www.kongisking.net*).

Blogger Dennis Mahoney urges bloggers to "offer something new" (*www.alistapart.com/articles/writebetter/*). But as the blogosphere grows exponentially, successful business bloggers will have to work much harder to contribute something unique to the blogosphere. Small, fast teams that can be first with targeted content will have the edge here.

Microformats

Blogs are great at presenting information that humans can read and understand. But there's a lot of buzz these days surrounding the possibility that blogs and Web pages could be formatted in a way that would make them easy for computers and other sites to read and understand as well.

Many experts think that this possibility could be realized by using *microformats* (*http://microformats.org*), shown in **Figure 9.2**, which provide an easy way for businesses and people to dynamically exchange data about things like inventory, product pricing, or even wedding gift registries. For example, one could "wrap" mentions of an inventory item in a microformat, and then other computers could easily recognize the data on the Web. The possibilities are endless, but the potential is only starting to be realized.

Figure 9.2

The Microformat blog includes news, code, and discussions about this promising new way to think about data on the Web.

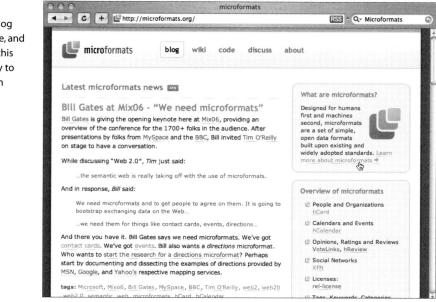

The acceptance of standards-based design—which we discussed in Chapter 4—has led to the widespread use of Web content that is structured in a clean, easy-to-understand way. Computers understand Web pages built in this logical fashion. Because standards-based pages are so cleanly built, code on a page could be made to contain descriptive information—such as "this is an inventory item"—that computers could easily understand. Many experts now believe that widespread agreement on descriptions and specifics of text structure could mean the creation of many new and useful ways to exchange data.

Imagine you own a restaurant, and you've posted about a new addition to your wine list on your blog. That may be great for Web surfers who happen to drop by and lay their eyes on the list. But wouldn't it be even better if their computer or PDA notified aficionados that their favorite wine has become available just down the street? This is the promise of microformats combined with RSS delivery. Your description of the new wine, "wrapped" with a little "wine list item" formatting could make it happen.

 NOTE: Microsoft has shown much interest in hCard and hCal, microformats for contact and calendar information, and has demoed them in an application called Live Clipboard that shares structured data between Web sites and desktop applications.

How? If each list item were "wrapped" in an agreed-upon, widely accepted and understood "wine list item" microformat, it would be easy for customers to be alerted when a wine they like is being offered nearby. Interested customers could tell their computer, cell phone, or PDA to monitor RSS "wine list item" feeds from local restaurants and to alert them when the 2003 Pere de Famille from Betz Family Winery appears. Another option would be to ask Technorati or Google what restaurants in a specific area code offer "wine list item" formatted content containing Chilean Cabernets.

Commenting on microformats, Bill Gates said that they're "going to bootstrap exchanging data on the Web.... [W]e need them for things like contact cards, events, [and] directions." We agree completely. The possibilities for e-commerce and online shopping applications are enormous. A company could publish an inventory list that could be dynamically read by the computers of suppliers. These suppliers could then automatically send the company more components as they are needed.

Mashups

The term *mashup* was originally used to describe what happens when a DJ creates an entirely new composition by taking the vocal track from one song and combining it with the instrumental track of another.

Just as DJs are inspired to blend musical compositions together, geeks are inspired to mix up Web-based applications. One useful mashup is Bus Monster (*www.busmonster.com*), which is the creation of Seattle-based Web entrepreneur Chris Smoak. He took Google Maps and combined it with the scheduling application generated by the local mass transit system to create a real-time bus locater that issues warnings when a user's bus is approaching. Another mashup can be seen in **Figure 9.3**.

Figure 9.3

Housingmaps.com is a mashup that combines data from Google Maps and Craigslist to give users geographical information about newly listed apartments.

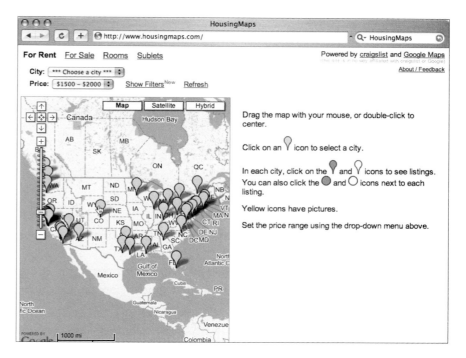

In the near future, companies will learn that they can drive traffic by creating mashups that add value to their sites. And just as interesting posts and content can build attention and discussion, interesting combinations of data provided by other sites can make your site a destination. What's more, the company that provides customers with a useful and popular mashup will create considerable goodwill for itself on the Web.

Take Nordstrom, for example. Their women's shoe department could cross-reference regional inventories with the styles and brands of shoes featured on television, in magazines, and on the runways. A user could see a pair of shoes she liked, go to the mashup, and find out instantly where they could be purchased and for what price.

When you consider that Web sites like Amazon, Google, eBay, and hundreds of others make all their data available for potential mashing, you'll begin to see that there are many thousands of potential applications for creative geeks to work on.

As is always the case with progress, the exception eventually evolves into the rule. Organizations that become early adopters, jumping into the Web headfirst and using their blogs and Web sites to creatively interact with stakeholders, are ahead of the curve and their competitors. Customers are often surprised and delighted with the flexibility, responsiveness, and community spirit of these companies.

But eventually, people will grow to expect this level of superior communication and flexibility. As blogging and related Web technologies become more common and more powerful, it's inevitable that companies that decide not to participate altogether will be left behind.

Mainstreamed and Mainlined

It's extremely difficult to predict the specific technologies that will catch on, or to know which technology standards will be widely embraced in the future. If we assembled a group of computer industry experts together in a room, they would debate endlessly over what the future will look like. Just a couple of years ago, few people would have predicted that blogs would become a phenomenon, and the global success of the iPod surprised many.

Despite this uncertainty, there is one thing all the gurus will agree on, and that's that all exotic new technologies eventually become boring commodities. Things we take for granted today (and don't pay much for) such as email, hard drives, and even radio started out as rare and expensive tools.

Old-timers can remember the mid-1990s when the covers of *Time, Fortune, Business Week,* and even *People* touted the wonders of the Web browser, which today is a free and unremarkable part of every computer user's day.

We largely don't think about the technology behind television, email, or the Web browser anymore. Instead we focus on the content being delivered with that technology. People used to say, "I use Netscape" or "Let's check the Internet." Now they focus on the sites they visit, not the technology used to get there.

Blogs and blogging will take the same route, and will simply become business as usual. As with the Web in general, the geeky early adopters jumped in long ago, and now we're seeing business professionals of all kinds coming into the game. The more participants we have, the less rarefied a forum it becomes.

Like everything else that was once revolutionary, blogs will eventually become yesterday's news. It doesn't mean they'll go away; it just means that they'll be commonplace. But as pioneer business blogger Anil Dash says, "Boring is good for business. Banks are boring, and look how well they do."

Publish and Prosper

While the competition for attention has heated up in the blogosphere, it will continue to serve as an ideal platform for online publishers for some time to come. As we said earlier, blogs will continue to be the easiest and least expensive way to deliver syndicated content. The syndication delivery platform will become incredibly pervasive over the next few years, and it seems clear that publishing to RSS and similar formats is becoming obligatory.

Blogs have become an effective way for businesses and individuals to communicate with customers, thanks to all the advantages offered by the technology. The key benefits to blogging (easy, inexpensive, powerful, syndicatable) will accelerate in the next few years, and so will the benefits to businesses that leverage these tools. Because of where blogging is now, and where it's likely headed, it's clear to us that the future belongs to the bloggers.

When we talk to businesspeople about blogging, we often find that many of them have substantial fear of the blogosphere. "What if people say bad things about us," they ask, "and what if we make a mistake?"

A lot of this fear comes from the telling and retelling of blogosphere horror stories, some of which we've shared with you in this book. But the reality is that it's very difficult to mess up catastrophically in the blogosphere. Because when it comes right down to it, bloggers are really very welcoming to businesses. All they really ask is that you share your perspective, engage with them, and show them that their thoughts and feelings about your business matter to you. In the end, that's all most customers really want—bloggers or not. And you're certainly capable of delivering that.

As an attendee at one of our seminars once told us, "The only fear I have about this stuff is the fear of the unknown." We hope that this book has cast light into the shadows for you and helped you to see that there's nothing to fear in the blogosphere if you are prepared to engage your core audience with an authentic, human voice.

So go out there. Become a blog geek. Meet your customers. Have a good time. Publish and prosper.

Index

Let Us Break Bread
TOGETHER

A Passover Haggadah for Christians

PASTOR MICHAEL SMITH
RABBI RAMI SHAPIRO

PARACLETE PRESS
BREWSTER, MASSACHUSETTS

Unless otherwise designated, the New Testament Scripture quotations are taken from the *New Revised Standard Version* of the Bible, © 1989, Division of Christian Education of the National Council of the Churches of Christ in the United States of America. Used by permission. All rights reserved.

Scripture quotations marked (NIV) are taken from the *Holy Bible, New International Version. NIV.* ©1973, 1978, 1984 by the International Bible Society. Used by permission of Zondervan Publishing House. All rights reserved.

Library of Congress Cataloging-in-Publication Data

Smith, Michael, 1954 Sept. 1-
Let us break bread together : a Passover Haggadah for Christians / Michael Smith, Rami Shapiro
   p. cm.
  ISBN 1-55725-444-3
  1. Passover—Christian observance. I. Shapiro, Rami M. II. Title.
  BV199.P25S63 2005
  265′.9—dc22

                     2004025204

2005 First printing

Published by Paraclete Press
Brewster, Massachusetts
www.paracletepress.com
Printed in the United States of America

Jesus said to his disciples,
"I have eagerly desired to eat this Passover with you . . ."
LUKE 22:15

TABLE OF CONTENTS

PREFACE

This small book is called a *haggadah*, Hebrew for "The Telling." It is the telling of the story of the Exodus of the Hebrew people from slavery in Egypt. The telling includes words and actions, using both mind and body to recall the horror of slavery and the joy of liberation. If you come to this haggadah at all familiar with the traditions of the Jewish Passover, you know that the bread of the title of this book refers to the unleavened bread, the matzah, that the Jews hurriedly baked in preparation for their exodus from Egypt. Breaking this matzah together has been a tribal and family ritual of the Jewish people for thousands of years. It is now finding its way into the homes and churches of Christians as well.

There are over two thousand versions of the Passover haggadah for Jews. This is not one of them. This is not a Jewish haggadah and is not meant for Jewish use. On the contrary, it is a Christian haggadah written explicitly for Christians in hopes of enriching their understanding of Passover.

For more and more churches and Christian families, the Passover seder (ritual Passover meal) is becoming a powerful opportunity to explore and honor the Jewishness of Jesus and the Jewish roots of Christianity. Yet the materials available to those Christians wishing to host a Passover seder are limited and often fail to explain the deeper meanings of the seder from either the Jewish or Christian perspectives. This haggadah addresses that need. It grew out of Rabbi Rami's personal experience at a church *seder* in Murfreesboro, Tennessee, where he now lives. As Rabbi Rami puts it:

> I was impressed by the sincerity of the participants but saddened at the inability of their haggadah to adequately explain Passover and to engage them in a manner that honored the Jewish faith and yet spoke directly to their faith as Christians. They did their best to follow the Jewish seder rituals but could not make them their own. I felt a need to help them understand Passover on a deeper level, and I knew this could best be done by creating a haggadah specifically addressed to Christians. Not being a Christian myself, I turned to my friend Mike Smith, pastor of the First Baptist Church of Murfreesboro. I felt certain we could collaborate to create a haggadah that would help Christians experience an authentic and meaningful Passover seder.

The haggadah you are reading is the result of that collaboration. We have labored in the context of friendship and mutual respect. Both of us are steeped in our respective religious traditions. We have no desire to blur the distinctions between those traditions or even to try to create a haggadah that might be used by both faiths. This is a Christian haggadah intended for use by Christians in their homes and churches.

In addition to its intended audience, another unique feature of our haggadah is that it follows a question-and-answer format. We chose this format for several reasons. First, asking questions is at the heart of both Judaism in general and the Jewish seder in particular. Second, asking and answering questions can serve as a catalyst for conversation among participants on the major themes of Passover: slavery, freedom, and one's personal relationship with God. Third, the format maximizes the opportunity for guests to participate in the seder. While there are sections of the haggadah designated for the LEADER and others for the

COMMUNITY as a whole, most of this haggadah is read by going around the table or room and inviting people to read the questions and answers in turn.

We hope that your participation will not end with the reading of the haggadah and that the questions wrestled with during the reading of the haggadah will set the tone for table discussion during the meal. While it is natural to engage in small talk, the seder is best experienced as an opportunity to seriously explore the reality of slavery and liberation in your life.

We have done our best to create a haggadah that honors the teachings of both Judaism and Christianity. Some in each of our faith traditions may conclude that we have failed, ought not to have undertaken such a task, or have created something a little dangerous. We feel the potential benefits outweigh the risks. As more and more Christians take on the Passover seder as part of their religious life, it will benefit everyone to do so not as an experience of the exotic, but as a way of enriching understanding and appreciation of Judaism even as Christians deepen their connection to Jesus.

Serious Jews and Christians have much to learn from one another. We do not have to become like one another in practice or belief to do so. In fact, exposure to our differences may help us grow in faith and understanding.

We hope our haggadah proves useful to individuals, families, and churches. Please feel free to adapt the haggadah as you see fit. We regard it as a task begun, not finished, and would welcome suggestions from our readers on how it might be improved.

May both faith and freedom deepen in your life.

Mike Smith, Pastor, First Baptist Church, Murfreesboro, Tennessee
Rami Shapiro, Rabbi, One River Foundation

ACKNOWLEDGMENTS

We might never have met except through the efforts of Jeff and Judy Fryer. They brought us together over meals, setting the stage for further conversations and a deepening friendship. Good introductions expand the circle of fellowship and make the world a better place. We would be remiss if we failed to take this opportunity to thank Jeff and Judy for their ministry of introduction.

Our thanks also go to the staff of Bangkok Café, a small Thai restaurant one block off the town square. Not only do they prepare excellent food, they also consistently provide a quiet, unrushed environment in which a Jewish rabbi and a Christian pastor can take the time to get to know one another. To find such an oasis of calm is a great blessing, and we are grateful.

Neither of us can begin to name all the teachers, writers, synagogue and church members, and mentors who have influenced us. Suffice it to say both of us have had the privilege of being influenced by men and women who consistently sought to foster meaningful dialogue between those of various faith traditions. They, of course, are not responsible for any errors of fact or perspective that may have crept into our work. Still, we probably would not have become the kind of persons who would listen well to one another without their influence.

Both of us have the good fortune to be sustained by spouses who encourage us in our work. We take this opportunity to thank them for their support and love.

A NOTE ON TRANSLATION

We quote from the Hebrew Scriptures, the Greek New Testament, and the Hebrew text of the traditional Jewish haggadah. Our English translations of the Greek come from both the New Revised Standard Version and the New International Version of the Bible. Our English translations of the Hebrew are Rabbi Rami's.

Translation is more art than science, and you might want to compare our renderings to other versions. Rabbi Rami's translations are intended to highlight the spiritual message of the Hebrew, and in this way to make the meaning of the text as clear as possible.

The one area in which we departed from conventional translations is the traditional Hebrew blessings over various foods. The Hebrew reads *Baruch Ata Adonai Eloheinu Melech haOlam* and is literally translated as *Blessed are you, Lord our God, sovereign of the universe.* . . . We have translated the formal *Lord our God* to *Abba,* Hebrew for "Father," a term better reflecting Jesus' understanding of his and our relationship with God.

Remember that Hebrew is read from right to left, rather than from left to right. This order is reversed in both the transliteration and, of course, in the English translations.

A NOTE TO THE LEADER

Coordinating a Passover seder is a big job! You are responsible for pulling together invitations, setup, food preparation and the reading of the haggadah. We have tried to make leading the seder as easy as possible. Even so, you may want to secure extra help with at least two parts of the seder experience.

The first of these is the invitation. If your church or family is used to holding a Passover seder, you may not need our advice, but if seder is a new practice for you and your community, we suggest you send a brief letter of explanation along with the formal invitation. The letter should highlight the following matters.

The Jewishness of Jesus
The centrality of the Passover seder in the life of Jews and, therefore, Jesus as a Jew
The universal application of the Passover message: liberation from the various slaveries that constrict our lives
The healing power that comes from sharing a sacred meal with family and friends

In addition to the letter and formal invitation, we think it wise to prepare your guests in two other ways as well.

First, encourage them to bring canned goods for donation to a soup kitchen or homeless shelter. The seder includes a specific time to mention such gifts of food, and you don't want people to feel left out because they did not know to bring a food donation. Second, the seder ends with children hunting for the *afikomen*, a broken piece of *matzah* hidden earlier in the service that, once found, represents healing and wholeness. The finder is rewarded with a gift. The gift should be monetary, and the money should then be donated to a cause of the child's choosing. To ensure that the children understand where their prize will go, you may want to explain that part of the seder in your letter of invitation and ask parents to discuss the matter in advance with their children. Parents of the child who finds the afikomen can then tell you where to send the donation. You should probably prepare a short list of possible recipients as well and include this along with your invitation.

THE CHRISTIAN-PASSOVER CONNECTION

Because Jesus was an observant Jew, Passover was a central part of his life. The Gospel According to Luke makes it very clear that Jesus celebrated Passover as a child: "Now every year his (Jesus') parents went to Jerusalem for the festival of the Passover" (Lk. 2:41). It also tells us that at the age of twelve Jesus caused his parents some worry: "When the festival was ended and they started to return, the boy Jesus stayed behind in Jerusalem, but his parents did not know it" (Lk. 2:43).

As in his early days, Passover played an important role in the life of Jesus in his last days.

> Then came the day of Unleavened Bread, on which the Passover lamb had to be sacrificed. So Jesus sent Peter and John, saying, "Go and prepare the Passover meal for us that we may eat it." They asked him, "Where do you want us to make preparations for it?" "Listen," he said to them, "when you have entered the city, a man carrying a jar of water will meet you; follow him into the house he enters and say to the owner of the house, 'The teacher asks you, "Where is the guest room, where I may eat the Passover with my disciples?"' He

will show you a large room upstairs, already furnished. Make preparations for us there." So they went and found everything as he had told them; and they prepared the Passover meal. (Lk. 22:7–13)

Jesus said to his disciples, "I have eagerly desired to eat this Passover with you before I suffer" (Lk. 22:15). *This Passover* refers to the seder; *with you* refers to all his disciples past and present. Observing the Passover seder is a way of continuing to honor this fervent wish of Jesus.

Jesus used this, his final Passover seder, as an opportunity to teach. During the seder Jesus asked his followers to "[d]o this in remembrance of me" (Lk. 22:19). While today we may interpret Jesus' words differently, the early church took him to be referring to the Passover seder, and made the seder central to Christianity for the next three hundred years.

There are other connections between Passover and the Church. Luke's Acts of the Apostles makes two references to the Festival of Unleavened Bread (Acts 12:3; 20:6), which is another name for the Jewish holy day of Passover. These passages link Peter and Paul to Passover services in Jerusalem and Greece, respectively.

The order of the Passover meal is the basis for the early church's Lord's Day worship called the Agape Feast and Eucharist. After the year 300 CE, the Agape Feast was separated from the Eucharist, and five Church Councils between 320 CE and 816 CE sought, albeit unsuccessfully, to eliminate the Agape Feast altogether. The Feast is still celebrated in the Greek Orthodox Church and in some denominations of Protestant Christianity as well.

Today, some seventeen hundred years later, renewed interest in the Jewishness of Jesus has led many Christians to reclaim the Passover seder as part of their heritage. Christian and Jewish seders, however, differ from one another. For Christians the Passover seder connects them to

Jesus the Jew and thus deepens their understanding of Jesus the Christ. For Jews the Passover seder is a global family reunion focusing on the retelling of the core story of the Jewish people: their liberation from slavery in Egypt. The Passover story is the key to Jewish self-understanding, leading as it does to receiving the revelation of God's Torah (the Five Books of Moses) at Mount Sinai, the confederation of the Hebrew tribes into a single people, and the ultimate settling of that people in the Promised Land of Israel.

While borrowing heavily from the original seder of the Jews, this Christian haggadah does not pretend to be in any way Jewish. Participants in this seder are not imitating the Jews, but learning from them.

It is the belief of both Dr. Smith and Rabbi Rami that by deepening our respective faiths and our understanding of each other's faith we will come to a common ground of respect for both the differences between us and the greater unity that surrounds us. We hope this haggadah contributes a bit to finding that common ground.

SETTING THE SEDER TABLE

The seder is a ritual meal and requires some formal preparation. Here are the items you will need and how to make them.

The Seder Plate. Because you may be new to hosting or leading a seder, we have paid special attention to the setup of the seder plate, a central part of the service itself.

The actual plate itself may be as simple as a paper plate or as fancy as a special seder plate purchased at a Judaica gift shop. If you plan to host an annual seder in your home you may prefer to purchase a plate especially designed for seder use. You can do this on-line or through a local synagogue gift shop. The advantage of the plate dedicated for the seder is both aesthetic and spiritual. Aesthetically such a plate can add to the special atmosphere of your seder table; spiritually it can make the nonverbal statement that this isn't an ordinary meal, but a holy feast.

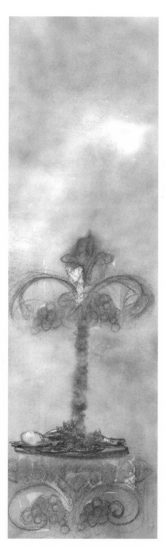

If you are hosting a large gathering, purchasing such plates is not practical, though you may opt to have one for the leader's table. Strong paper or plastic plates will do just fine, and it is a good idea to have one at each table so that people can see what the seder is referring to as the service makes reference to each item on the plate. If yours is a church seder, you might ask the children in your church school to decorate plates that will be used at the community seder. Teachers can use this exercise as an opportunity to talk about Passover and the seder, and to explain the different symbols to the students in advance of the meal. Regardless of the kind of plate you use, the plate itself will hold six items:

Charoset. *Charoset* is a mixture of apples, nuts, red wine or grape juice, and spices, and symbolizes the mortar the Jewish slaves made in their building pyramids for Pharaoh. To make charoset, you will need 1 cup of walnuts, 1 Granny Smith green apple, 2 tsp. cinnamon, 2 tsp. sugar (optional), and red wine or grape juice to moisten. Chop the nuts and apples to the consistency you want. Mix in the spices, and moisten with wine or grape juice. The texture of the charoset should remind you of mortar, so do not make it smooth or buttery.

Zeroa. *Zeroa* is a roasted shank bone of a lamb or neck of a chicken. Zeroa is symbolic of the Paschal lamb offered as the Passover sacrifice in Temple days. From a Christian perspective it is symbolic of Jesus, "For Christ, our Passover lamb, has been sacrificed for us," (1 Cor. 5:7 NIV). You can purchase a shank bone or chicken neck at most butcher shops. Wrap the shank bone in foil and roast it in the oven for about thirty minutes. Zeroa is a symbol only and is not eaten during the Passover meal.

Baytza. *Baytza* is an egg, first hard-boiled and then roasted. The hard-boiled egg was a reminder of the festival sacrifice held at the Temple in Jerusalem. With the destruction of the Temple (first by the Babylonians in 586 BCE and later by the Romans in 70 CE), the Jews began to associate the hard-boiled egg with mourning the loss of their Temple. Today the egg reminds all of us to mourn the suffering of all peoples trapped in the horrors of slavery.

Karpas. *Karpas* is a green vegetable, usually parsley, and represents the reemergence of life at springtime. During the seder the karpas is dipped in saltwater and eaten, so make sure you have a small sprig of parsley for each guest. The saltwater represents the tears of suffering that become tears of joy when we move from slavery to freedom.

Maror. *Maror* is bitter herbs, usually horseradish root or prepared horseradish. Maror represents the bitterness of life lived under slavery. You can buy prepared horseradish at most grocery stores.

Saltwater. In addition to these food items, the seder plate holds a small dish of saltwater in which the *karpas*/parsley is dipped. If your plate can't hold the saltwater, a separate dish is fine.

While preparing the seder plate is not a huge ordeal, it may take an hour. It is wise to prepare the plate in advance. Allowing children to help is another fun way to get them involved in learning about Passover and in feeling some investment in the success of the meal.

As you prepare each item invite the children to talk about slavery. You may choose to focus on ways in which they are trapped and enslaved. Slavery is not something that younger children understand right away. Talk with them about habits they cannot seem to break. Older children can explore how they can get enslaved to feelings and expectations, and how our consumer society tries to enslave them to certain brands and logos. Make sure to talk about ways they can maintain their freedom from such slavery.

Matzah. *Matzah* does not go on the seder plate itself. You can purchase a special three-tiered matzah plate to hold the three pieces of matzah needed for the seder. Any plate wide enough to hold the matzah will do, however. While the seder requires three pieces of matzah, have extra matzah on hand since lots of matzah may be consumed during the meal. A separate plate provided to hold the three pieces of matzah used in the seder is covered by a cloth or napkin.

Matzah is the unleavened bread that the Israelites took with them when they escaped from Egypt. The Bible tells us that the people had no time to bake leavened bread, and had to settle for matzah instead. It is also true that matzah is lighter than bread, easier to carry, and lasts longer then regular bread.

If you go to your local supermarket to purchase matzah for your seder you may notice that some boxes will say the matzah inside is kosher for Passover, while some boxes will say the matzah is not kosher for Passover. *Kosher* is the Hebrew word for "fit." Matzah is fit for Passover only if the grain used to make the matzah has been protected from dampness prior to baking, and baked in a hurry (about eighteen minutes). The concern here is that the dough used for the matzah, if allowed to dampen will produce yeast or leaven, and leavened products are prohibited to Jews during the week of Passover.

The Hebrew word for leavened products is *chumetz*, and Jews observing Passover abstain from eating anything that contains chumetz. In addition they remove all leavened products from their homes. The idea is to spend one week leaven-free. Why? Because leavened breads were made with sour dough, chumetz came to represent all the things we do that bring slavery and sourness into our lives and the lives of those with whom we come into contact. Avoiding chumetz is a challenge to weed out sourness and enslavement during the Passover week, and to stop living soured and enslaved lives. This is a challenge all of us can appreciate and make our own.

As a Christian you may choose not to concern yourself with the details of kosher and unkosher matzah, and while you may choose to eat chumetz during Passover, and even at your seder, the presence of matzah is still a reminder of the deeper work of this holy week. As Jesus taught, "[I]t is not what goes into the mouth that defiles a person, but it is what comes out of the mouth that defiles" (Mt. 15:11).

In addition to the matzah eaten at the seder it is customary to eat soup with matzah balls. To make matzah balls you need 4 eggs, 1 cup of matzah meal, and a pinch of salt. Beat the egg yolks and salt together. Beat the egg whites separately until they are very stiff. Fold the egg yolks and egg whites together, and add the matzah meal. Roll the mixture into balls and drop them into rapidly boiling salted water in a very large pot. Boil for forty-five minutes with the pot covered.

The Afikomen. Another aspect of the seder you may choose to prepare in advance is the *afikomen*, or "dessert." We mentioned earlier that this was a piece of matzah hidden during the service and sought out by the children toward the end of the meal. Technically the seder cannot be concluded without eating the afikomen.

During the seder the middle of the three pieces of matzot is broken in half and the smaller half is hidden away. The challenge to you as leader is this: if the children know the afikomen is to be hidden, and that they will be asked to find it, and that there is a prize for doing so, they will never take their eyes off of you, making it very difficult for you to hide the afikomen. Here are two ways to get around this.

First, you could hide the afikomen in advance of the meal. While technically incorrect, it does solve the problem. Second, you can ask another adult to do the hiding on your behalf. While the children are focused on you, your surrogate can hide the afikomen undetected. Whoever hides the afikomen should make sure it can be found, but not too easily. If you have lots of children at your seder you may wish to hide more than one piece of matzah.

A word about wine. It is traditional to drink four cups of wine during a Passover seder. Grape juice is a fine substitute for those for whom wine is inappropriate. Make sure you have enough of one or the other for the entire seder.

Elijah's Cup. In addition to the four cups of wine or grape juice that you will drink at your seder, there is a fifth cup, filled only at the conclusion of the seder. This cup is called *Kos Eliyahu*, or Elijah's Cup. Judaism teaches that Elijah, who is called the Prophet of Peace, will come to announce the coming of the Messiah. Jesus, too, makes reference to Elijah. His disciples ask him, "Why do the scribes say that Elijah must come first [before the Messiah]?" Jesus said to them, "Elijah is indeed coming first to restore all things" (Mk. 9:11-12). Toward the conclusion of the seder Elijah's Cup is filled and the doors to the home or church are opened to allow the spirit of Elijah to enter. Elijah makes his presence known by taking a sip of wine from the *Kos Eliyahu*.

There need be only one Elijah's Cup at your seder, most likely placed at the table of the seder leader. When the Cup is filled and the doors are opened, invite the children to gather around the Cup to see if Elijah does in fact take a sip. You might invite the youngest children to drink a bit from the Cup as well to honor Elijah's visit and thus ensuring that the wine or grape juice in the Cup does indeed decrease.

A pillow. It is customary for the leader to recline on a pillow during the seder as a sign that this is a meal of free and fearless people. The pillow is referenced during the seder and you may wish to have a small one on hand to symbolize the free nature of this gathering.

THE SEDER

LEADER'S WELCOME

LEADER

"How very good and pleasant it is when kindred live together in unity." (Ps. 133:1)

Tonight we sit in special fellowship, honoring each other and God with a Passover meal. We do so for at least three reasons. First, Jesus celebrated Passover, and our Passover links us to him and to the ancient Jewish roots of our own faith. Second, the celebration of freedom, which is at the heart of Passover, is universal, inspiring people of different faiths and even people aligned with no faith to labor for liberation. Third, the personal challenge of Passover—freeing ourselves from personal enslavements of thought, word, and deed—may benefit all of us.

If we are to benefit from our Passover seder, however, we must be authentic in what we are doing. We must not simply imitate the Passover of our Jewish neighbors. Instead we must engage in our own spiritual liberation. Our seder, therefore, is not an imitation but an adaptation. We draw from Judaism but we do not pretend to be Jews. In this way, we may learn from our deepest historical roots yet remain true to ourselves and our faith.

Our meal is called a *seder*, from the Hebrew term for "order." The Book of Genesis tells us that God orders all creation. Though we affirm this is so, we must confess we often cannot sense God's ordering presence. Our own habit of trying to control things for ourselves gets in the way. Paradoxically, the more we seek to control things, the more they spin out of control.

The story we tell on Passover is one of human control and divine liberation. Egypt symbolizes our enslavement to power, the kind of bondage that results from our seeking to control our own lives. Pharaoh symbolizes our addiction to power and to the need to control. The Jewish people symbolize all of us who are enslaved in some fashion to the ego's need to control. The entire Passover meal is a celebration of our rediscovery of God's order and the liberation that comes when we refocus our attention on the only thing we can control: our decision to surrender control of our lives to God.

To that end let us pray: O Lord of all creation and of each human life, hear now our prayer. As we gather about this table, relive the story of the Exodus, and partake of the food provided, we ask that you use the occasion toward your ends. May our felt need for you be deepened, our bonds with one another be tightened, our willingness to surrender to your rule be strengthened, and our ministry to others be extended. Amen.

CANDLE LIGHTING

[Each table should have two white candles that are lighted for Passover.]

LEADER

"Let your light shine before others, so that they may see your good works and give glory to your Father in heaven" (Mt. 5:16).

LEADER

We begin our seder with the making of light. Yet light makes sense only in contrast to darkness. Take a moment to recall and embrace the dark times of your life: times of confusion, depression, and loss. Allow yourself to feel the "Dark Night of the Soul" not as punishment for sin but as prelude to salvation: "there was evening, there was morning, a first day" (Gen. 1:5).

[The candles are lighted while the participants' eyes are closed.]

Now open your eyes and behold the light as a gift from the One who says "Light" and light comes into being.

COMMUNITY

בָּרוּךְ אַתָּה יְיָ, אֱלֹהֵינוּ מֶלֶךְ הָעוֹלָם,
אֲשֶׁר קִדְּשָׁנוּ בְּמִצְוֹתָיו
וְצִוָּנוּ לְהַדְלִיק נֵר שֶׁל יוֹם טוֹב:

Baruch Ata Adonai Eloheinu melech haolam, asher kidshanu b'mitzvotav v'tzivanu l'hadleek nair shel yom tov.

Bless you, Abba, Sovereign of all life, who honors us with the opportunity to kindle the light of freedom.

QUESTION

What does it mean to be free? Is freedom simply a matter of doing what we wish whenever we wish?

ANSWER

There is a difference between independence and freedom. As a child matures she learns to say no to the will of others. This is the beginning of her independence. As she grows she adds to this no a yes affirming her desires and will. Many of us never mature beyond this point. We call this freedom, but it is only independence. True freedom comes when we can also say no to our own desires and yes to the needs and desires of others. True freedom arises not when we do our will but when we do God's will: doing justly, acting compassionately, and walking humbly (Mic. 6:8).

THE SYMBOLS OF PASSOVER

LEADER

To help us understand the meaning of our seder as a whole, we explore the meaning of each part.

QUESTION

What is the meaning of the roasted shank bone?

ANSWER

The shank bone, called *zeroa*, reminds us of the Paschal lamb offered to God by the Jews. For us Christians it calls to mind the significance of Jesus, whom we remember as God's Paschal Lamb offered on our behalf.

QUESTION

What is the meaning of the boiled egg?

ANSWER

For many Jews and Christians the egg, *baytza* in Hebrew, symbolizes the circle of life and death and the turning of the seasons. Passover, like Easter, is a spring holy day. In the Jewish tradition, Passover marks the renewal of life in the natural world. Christians inevitably are reminded of the resurrection of Jesus. In Judaism the egg is also considered a sign of mourning, reminding us to honor the suffering of those trapped in slavery, both the enslaved and the enslavers, and, as Christians, to honor the Passion of our Lord whose suffering was the key to our liberation.

QUESTION

What is the meaning of the bitter herbs?

ANSWER

The herbs are called *maror*, "bitter," and are eaten to remind us of the bitter taste of slavery in all its forms.

QUESTION

What is the meaning of the mixture of nuts, apples, and spices?

ANSWER

This is *charoset* and symbolizes the mortar the Hebrew slaves used to build the pyramids of Egypt. It reminds us all of the great yet ultimately futile works to which so many individuals and societies are enslaved.

QUESTION

What is the meaning of the parsley on our seder plate?

ANSWER

This is called *karpas* and represents hope. Later in our seder we will dip the karpas in saltwater, symbolizing the sadness of slavery, the joy of liberation, and the effort needed to move from the first to the second. Hope must lead to action if our desire for liberation is to become the reality of freedom.

QUESTION

What is the meaning of the unleavened bread?

ANSWER

Matzah has many meanings. It is called the "Bread of Affliction", reminding us when we eat it of the suffering of the poor. It is flat to remind us not to become puffed up but instead to remain simple and humble. It is dry to remind us that we cannot live by bread alone, that we need the Water of Life that is God. Matzah for Passover is prepared under strict supervision of rabbis whose job is to make sure the dough does not sour and rise. For this reason when we eat matzah we are reminded to root out the sourness in our lives and the sourness we bring to the lives of others.

QUESTION

Why are there three *matzot* on the table?

ANSWER

The number three is sacred in both Judaism and Christianity. In Judaism it may represent the three pillars of Judaism: God, Torah, and Israel; the three pillars of civilization: revelation, divine worship, and acts of loving kindness; and thought, word, and deed—what Judaism refers to as the "Three Garments of the Soul"—the three primary ways we engage each other and the world. For Christians, the three matzot may symbolize the completeness of God's saving work: the calling out of God's special people, the extension of God's grace to the Gentiles, and the promise of a new heaven and earth in which God's people will dwell. The number is also special to Christians as a representation of the three persons of the Trinity: God the Father, God the Son, and God the Holy Spirit.

QUESTION

Why is so much wine or grape juice needed?

ANSWER

It is traditional for guests to drink four cups of wine or grape juice at a seder. The number four reminds us of four aspects of liberation mentioned by God in Exodus 6:6-7: "I shall take you from under your burdens"; "I shall rescue you"; "I shall redeem you"; and "I shall take you unto myself."

QUESTION

How might we understand "I shall take you from under your burdens"?

ANSWER

Some burdens are so heavy as to leave us feeling crushed. We cannot push them away. Only God can snatch us safely from beneath such burdens.

QUESTION

How might we understand "I shall rescue you"?

ANSWER

Our attachments are sometimes so strong we cannot pull ourselves loose. It is then that we must await God's rescue, allowing his power to replace our own.

QUESTION

How might we understand "I shall redeem you"?

ANSWER

Our enslavement to wrongful habits robs us of joy and hope. We cannot redeem ourselves because it is to ourselves that we are enslaved. Only God can redeem us and free us from captivity.

QUESTION

How might we understand "I shall take you unto myself"?

ANSWER

Our primary enslavement is to self and selfishness. True freedom comes when we surrender our small self to God and allow God to take us into his far greater Self.

QUESTION

What is the purpose of the extra empty wine cup?

ANSWER

This is call *Kos Eliyahu*, the Cup of the Prophet Elijah. The Bible tells us that Elijah never died, but was taken directly to heaven. Jewish tradition says Elijah returns to earth regularly to help people in need. On Passover it is said he visits every seder and shares a bit of drink with the guests to remind us that God never abandons us. Elijah is also the Prophet of Peace who will herald the coming of the Messiah. For Jews this will be seen as the first coming of the Messiah; for Christians it will be seen as the second coming. Offering a place at our table for Elijah reminds us to offer a place in our hearts for redemption.

QUESTION
What is the meaning of the saltwater?

ANSWER
The saltwater has three meanings. First, it represents the tears of sadness that are shed in slavery. Second, it symbolizes the tears of joy that flow at the moment of liberation. Third, it reminds us of the effort and sweat that go into moving from the first to the second.

LEADER
There is a great deal to remember about our Passover seder. Our hope is that the perspectives we have offered will enrich your experience of the meal. We trust that these questions will spark further questions, which will inform our conversation as we eat. Remember, it is in the spirit of Passover to ask questions. There are no wrong answers. The only mistake you can make is to pass up the opportunity to ask, explore, and share. All we ask is that your conversation be informed by the teaching of Jesus at his final seder, "I give you a new commandment, that you love one another. Just as I have loved you, you also should love one another. By this everyone will know that you are my disciples, if you have love for one another" (Jn. 13:34-35).

To that end let us pray: "O, God, teach us to trust you enough to ask the questions we have. Free us from the need to be perceived as clever or informed. Take the elements of the meal and use them to spark our curiosity, open our minds, intrigue our hearts, and deepen our capacity for love. Amen."

קַדֵּשׁ
Kadesh
FIRST CUP OF WINE

[*It is customary for the guests to fill each other's glasses and not their own.*]

QUESTION

Why do we fill each other's glasses and not our own?

ANSWER

The rabbis teach: What is the difference between heaven and hell? In both, the souls of the departed sit at long tables lavishly prepared with the finest foods. In both, the departed are made to eat with forks too long to allow them to feed themselves. In hell each soul struggles alone to ease a growing hunger. In heaven each soul feeds the soul sitting across the table and in this way all souls are full. Filling each other's glasses brings a taste of heaven to our table; it is a way of welcoming each other and affirming our desire to welcome all humanity to our table-fellowship. It also a reminder of God's commandment to love our neighbor as ourselves (Lev. 19:18; Mt. 19:19).

LEADER

The first cup binds us together in fellowship. We fill each other's cups as we hope to fill each other's hearts. In sharing this drink and meal we remind ourselves of our common bond as children of God.

rei — p'-ri ha-ga - fen.

COMMUNITY

בָּרוּךְ אַתָּה יְיָ, אֱלֹהֵינוּ מֶלֶךְ הָעוֹלָם,
בּוֹרֵא פְּרִי הַגָּפֶן:

Baruch Ata Adonai Eloheinu melech haolam borai pri hagaphen.

Bless you, Abba, Sovereign of all life, who births the fruit of the vine.

וּרְחַץ
Urchatz
WASHING THE HANDS

[The leader washes his or her hands on behalf of the community as a symbolic act of preparation for leading the community through the seder meal.]

QUESTION

Why do we wash our hands before continuing with our seder?

ANSWER

Washing the hands reminds us that we are entering a sacred space. The rabbis taught that with the destruction of the Temple in Jerusalem and the ending of sacrifice, the dinner table became the new altar, the central place of communing with God. Jesus, too, made Table-Fellowship a central act of his ministry. This banquet, each table around which we sit, is a tabernacle to God. Let us cleanse our hearts and minds even as we cleanse our hands.

כַּרְפַּס
Karpas
BLESSING THE GREEN VEGETABLE

[*Dip the parsley in the saltwater, but do not eat it.*]

QUESTION
Why is the parsley dipped in the saltwater?

ANSWER
Karpas, or green vegetable, symbolizes hope and renewal. The saltwater reminds us of the sweat of the brow, the hard work required if our hopes are to be realized in our lives. The first food we taste at our seder is the food of hope and work.

COMMUNITY

בָּרוּךְ אַתָּה יְיָ, אֱלֹהֵינוּ מֶלֶךְ הָעוֹלָם,
בּוֹרֵא פְּרִי הָאֲדָמָה:

Baruch Ata Adonai Eloheinu ruach haolam borai pri ha-adamah.
Bless you, Abba, Sovereign of all life, who births the fruit of the earth.

[*The karpas is now eaten.*]

יַחַץ
Yachatz
BREAKING THE MIDDLE MATZAH

[One participant at each table, or the leader at the head table, takes the middle of the three pieces of matzah and breaks it in two. Replace the smaller piece between the two unbroken pieces. Wrap the larger piece in a napkin. This will serve as the afikomen, the "dessert." At some point during the seder the afikomen is hidden for the children to find. The afikomen is eaten at the conclusion of the meal.]

QUESTION
Why do we use three pieces of matzah at our Passover seder?

ANSWER
The number three is sacred in both Judaism and Christianity. For Jews it refers to the three pillars of Judaism: God, Torah and Israel; the three pillars of civilization: wisdom, worship, and love; and the three pillars of human individuality: thought, word, and deed. For Christians, the number three symbolizes the Holy Trinity of Father, Son, and Holy Spirit; and the completeness of God's saving work: the calling out of his special people, the extension of his grace to the Gentiles, and the promise of a new heaven and earth in which his people will dwell.

QUESTION
Why is the middle matzah broken?

ANSWER

For the Jews the broken matzah is the matzah of speech. It is broken because our words are often used to hurt rather than heal and make whole. For Christians the broken matzah is the Son, who died on the cross that we might be saved.

QUESTION

Why do we hide this broken matzah?

ANSWER

There are two reasons. First, we hide half the matzah to remind ourselves how difficult it can be to find the right words to heal the hurts we create in our own and in others' hearts. Second, we hide it in order to remind us to seek God whenever we ourselves are feeling broken and lost. Our hope is that by sharing this meal with each other we begin to find the words of healing and to support each other's search for God.

LEADER

Matzah is called *lachma anya*, the "Bread of Affliction." It is the flat bread of those whose lives have been flattened by suffering and oppression. As you eat this bit of matzah, focus on your God-given kinship with all such men, women, and children. In this way you will awaken thoughts of compassion. Your words will naturally turn toward kindness, and your deeds toward justice.

LEADER

[*Uncover the matzah and lift the plate before the guests.*] This is the bread of suffering, reminding us of the dryness of a soul starved of hope. This is the bread of the broken, reminding us that no one is whole unless all are whole, for in the end we are one body, and when one part of the body aches the entire body suffers.

COMMUNITY

Let all who are hungry share this meal with us. Let all who are enslaved share this meal with us. Let all who are in need share this meal with us. Let all who are in *Mitzraim* share this meal with us.

QUESTION

What does the word *Mitzraim* mean?

ANSWER

Mitzraim is the Hebrew word for Egypt, but it means much more than that. In Hebrew *mitzraim* literally means "the narrow places"; Egypt is symbolic of the narrow places in which we find ourselves enslaved.

QUESTION

Can one who is a Christian be enslaved?

ANSWER

Yes. Jesus said, "You cannot serve God and wealth" (Mt. 6:24), and yet so many of us try to do so. To the extent we serve God we are free; to the extent we serve wealth we are enslaved. There is always a place of enslavement, always a narrow place from which we need to free ourselves. Sharing the bread of enslavement as part of this feast of freedom reminds us that liberation is not once and for all, but is instead an ongoing effort.

QUESTION

How are we to invite all who are hungry to share in this meal?

ANSWER

The call to feed the hungry is a call to action. Our meal is filled with symbols, but it is not itself symbolic. We eat real food and fill real stomachs. At this point in our service, we remind ourselves of the hunger that plagues so many in the world. But it is not enough to remember; we must also act. This is why we were asked to bring canned goods with us to our seder that we might help feed those in need.

QUESTION

Why do we mention both the hungry and the needy?

ANSWER

There is physical hunger and spiritual hunger. Even if our stomachs are filled, our hearts may be empty. This is why Jesus said people shall "not live by bread alone" (Mt. 4:4, quoting Deut. 8:3). How many of us hunger for love, companionship, community, or meaning? Just as we share our food, let us share our hearts as well, taking care to turn our talk to matters of the spirit.

מַגִּיד
Maggid
TELLING THE STORY
THE FOUR QUESTIONS

LEADER

Our seder is a time for asking and answering questions.
Four specific questions have been asked for centuries.

READER

How is this night different from other nights?

COMMUNITY

On all other nights we eat leavened or unleavened
bread, but tonight we eat only unleavened bread.

READER

Why on this night do we eat bitter herbs?

COMMUNITY

To remind us of the bitterness of slavery.

READER

Why on this night do we dip parsley into saltwater
and *matzah* into the *charoset* (apple and nut mixture)?

COMMUNITY

The first reminds us of the bitter taste of slavery. The
second reminds us of the sweet taste of freedom.

READER

Why on this night do we eat reclining on a pillow?

ANSWER

In ancient times only the free were allowed to recline at meals. We are relaxed in the company of our friends, eating without fear, and knowing that in this meal all are welcome as they are.

LEADER

O God, we live in a world in which slavery is real and takes many forms. While we may not have experienced political or physical slavery, we confess we have known and know what it means to be imprisoned by poor decisions, unhealthy attachments and dependencies, and sin itself. We remember as well that in Christ you have granted us freedom if only we will accept and use the gift. Tonight help us to know afresh the good taste of freedom and to resolve to live free in you.

THE FOUR QUESTIONERS

LEADER

There are four kinds of questioners: the wise, the foolish, the simple, and the one who knows not what to ask. Each speaks with a different voice: the voices of Wisdom, Doubt, Inquiry, and Faith.

The wise one asks, "What is the meaning of Passover?" This is the Voice of Wisdom that knows our connection with God and seeks to deepen it.

The foolish one asks, "Why do you bother with all of this?" This is the Voice of Doubt that separates us from each other and from God.

The simple one asks, "What do these foods mean, and why do we share them?" This is the Voice of Inquiry that wishes to bring us closer to truth.

The child too young to ask is the Voice of Faith, using silence to invite the telling of our story and the Good News it contains.

THE STORY OF THE EXODUS

[You may choose to shorten the story and sing Let My People Go.]

Let My People Go

We need not always weep and mourn,
Let my people go.
And wear these slavery chains forlorn,
Let my people go!
Refrain

O let us all from bondage flee,
Let my people go.
And soon may all this world be free,
Let my people go!
Refrain

LEADER

Thousands of years ago a great famine struck the Middle East. Only Egypt had food, for at the counsel of the Hebrew man Joseph, Egypt's Pharaoh had stockpiled food in advance of the famine. He sold the food back to his people and impoverished them. The Egyptians rebelled against this Pharaoh and established a new Pharaoh who enslaved the Hebrew people.

The new Pharaoh feared the Hebrews might lead a revolt against him, and he ordered the midwives to kill all boy babies born to Hebrew mothers. The midwives refused. Pharaoh then ordered his soldiers to raid the Hebrew camps and murder the baby boys.

One Hebrew mother, Yochabed, hid her son in a basket she had turned into a little boat and floated him down the Nile River where he might be found and rescued. She sent the boy's sister, Miriam, to follow the basket to see what became of her brother.

Pharaoh's daughter found the boy. She recognized the baby as a Hebrew, yet her love for life was greater than her fear of Pharaoh, and she raised him as her own son in the Pharaoh's court. Miriam spoke to the princess and offered her mother as a nurse for the boy, whom the princess called Moses. So Moses was raised by two mothers in the House of Pharaoh: the one who gave him life, and the one who saved it.

Being raised as a prince in Egypt, Moses could have turned his back on the fate of the slaves, but his two mothers saw to it that he would not. Both had risked their lives to protect his life, and both would teach him the value of life and the freedom to live it in service to God, compassion, justice, and truth.

One day Moses saw a slave being beaten by a guard. Moses tried to stop the guard and accidentally killed him. Moses hoped the deed would remain secret. When word got out that he had sided with the Hebrew slaves against the Egyptian guards, he fled Egypt to save his life. He ran to Midian where he married Zipporah, the daughter of Jethro, the priest.

Moses was happy in Midian tending Jethro's sheep and raising a family. But God had other plans for the Hebrew prince of Egypt. As Moses was shepherding his flock he saw a bush on fire. He went to investigate and found that the bush burned but was not burned up. God had gotten Moses's attention and spoke to him.

He commanded Moses to return to Egypt and free the slaves. Moses hesitated. He wanted nothing more to do with Egypt and Pharaoh. But in the end he agreed to go, joining with his brother, Aaron, and sister, Miriam, to liberate the slaves.

Moses tried to reason with Pharaoh but was ignored. Pharaoh saw himself as a god and doubted the power of Moses's God. Nine times God brought terrible plagues upon Egypt to convince Pharaoh to free the slaves. But Pharaoh refused. In the end God visited upon Pharaoh and Egypt the same kind of horror Pharaoh had visited upon the Hebrews: the death of the firstborn.

God told Moses to warn the Hebrew people to prepare for liberation. They were to bake flat breads called matzah that could be made quickly and packed in bulk. They were to sacrifice a lamb and smear some of its blood on the doorposts of their homes to mark them as slave quarters. The Angel of Death would pass over these marked houses and spare the firstborn within them. The horror of this plague broke Pharaoh's spirit, and he let the slaves go. But his anger against them rekindled, and he ordered his army to slaughter the Hebrews when they reached the shore of the Red Sea. God parted the waters and the Hebrew people escaped. Pharaoh's army raced after them, but as the last of the Hebrews reached safety, the waters closed about the Egyptians and they drowned.

The ex-slaves rejoiced at the death of their oppressors, but God called to them saying, "How dare you rejoice? The Egyptians are also my children. There is no joy in this. The cost of freedom is high. Respect it always."

In the spirit of compassion for the fallen Egyptians it is customary at every seder to spill out drops of wine for each plague they suffered. In this way we diminish our inappropriate joy at their suffering.

[*The plagues are read aloud, and using the pinky of your right hand you remove drops of wine from your cup and sprinkle them on a separate plate or napkin.*]

דָּם. צְפַרְדֵּעַ. כִּנִּים. עָרוֹב. דֶּבֶר. שְׁחִין.
בָּרָד. אַרְבֶּה. חֹשֶׁךְ. מַכַּת בְּכוֹרוֹת:

Dahm/Blood	*Tzfardeya*/Frogs	*Kinim*/Lice
Arov/Beasts	*Dever*/Mad Cow	*Sh'chin*/Boils
Barad/Hail	*Arbeh*/Locusts	*Choshech*/Darkness

Makat b'chorot//Death of the First Born

דַּיֵּנוּ:
Dayyenu
IT IS ENOUGH

[Dayyenu—*pronounced* die-ay-nu— *affirms that any gift from God is sufficient and that we do not ask anything from God but that which God desires us to have. The Leader says each verse and the community responds with* dayyenu, *"it is enough." Some groups may prefer to sing the Doxology.*]

LEADER

Dayyenu means "it is enough." We read this to remember all the gifts God gives and to cultivate an attitude of gratitude.

If the Jews escaped from Egypt but the sea had not opened—*Dayyenu*

If the sea had opened but they didn't find manna in the desert—*Dayyenu*

If they found the manna but did not receive the Sabbath—*Dayyenu*

If they received the Sabbath but did not receive the Torah—*Dayyenu*

If they received Torah but not the wisdom to understand her—*Dayyenu*

If they received wisdom but did not receive the Land of Israel—*Dayyenu*

If they received Israel but didn't build the Temple in Jerusalem—*Dayyenu*

If they built the Temple but didn't heed the call of the prophets—*Dayyenu*

While it is a good thing to say *dayyenu* and be satisfied with the gifts from God, it is another thing to be satisfied with ourselves. If we wish to be truly free, there is much in our world to which we must say *Lo Dayyenu*, "it is not enough."

If we love ourselves, but not our neighbors—	*Lo Dayyenu*
If we love our neighbors, but not our enemies—	*Lo Dayyenu*
If we end all war, but not starvation—	*Lo Dayyenu*
If we end starvation, but not illiteracy—	*Lo Dayyenu*
If we end illiteracy, but do not protect freedom of speech—	*Lo Dayyenu*
If we protect speech, but do not educate discerning minds—	*Lo Dayyenu*
If we were to educate the mind, but not the heart—	*Lo Dayyenu*
If we were to educate the heart, but not the soul—	*Lo Dayyenu*
If we were to educate the soul, but not the spirit—	*Lo Dayyenu*

THE SECOND CUP OF WINE
[Guests fill each other's cups.]

LEADER

Wine is a symbol of our joy, but it can also be the means of our enslavement. In like fashion, we can become drunk on our own power and intoxicated by the power of others, no longer seeing that only God is Lord. It is for this reason that we preface each cup of wine with a blessing, reminding ourselves to see through the delusion of self-power to the truth of God's power. Jesus said, "[E]veryone who commits sin is a slave to sin," (Jn. 8:34). Our second cup of wine is in honor of freedom. May all who drink it this night move away from sin and slavery toward freedom.

COMMUNITY:

בָּרוּךְ אַתָּה יְיָ, אֱלֹהֵינוּ מֶלֶךְ הָעוֹלָם,
בּוֹרֵא פְּרִי הַגָּפֶן:

Baruch Ata Adonai Eloheinu Melech haOlam borai pri hagaphen.
Bless you, Abba, Sovereign of all life, who births the fruit of the vine.

מוֹצִיא מַצָּה
Motzi Matzah
BLESSING OVER THE MATZAH

LEADER

We are now about to give thanks to God for the matzah and begin the eating of our Passover meal.

QUESTION

What is the significance of matzah?

ANSWER

Matzah is unleavened bread. In ancient times leaven was made from sour dough. Matzah is bread without sourness. During the weeklong observance of Passover, Jews abstain from all leavened products, called *chumetz*. Chumetz symbolizes sourness and the selfishness that causes it. We eat matzah as a reminder to examine our lives that we might stay free from sourness.

The unexamined life is leavened by self-importance, self-righteousness, and self-satisfaction. We honor Passover by seeking to free ourselves from these acts of *chumetz*. Indeed, we Christians may find this focus a natural conclusion to the long season of Lent, with its call to discern and repent of the sins that enslave us to evil.

COMMUNITY

בָּרוּךְ אַתָּה יְיָ, אֱלֹהֵינוּ מֶלֶךְ הָעוֹלָם,
הַמוֹצִיא לֶחֶם מִן הָאָרֶץ:

Baruch Ata Adonai Eloheinu Melech haOlam ha motzi lechem min ha-aretz.

Bless you, Abba, Sovereign of all life, through Whom the earth gives rise to bread.

בָּרוּךְ אַתָּה יְיָ, אֱלֹהֵינוּ מֶלֶךְ הָעוֹלָם,
אֲשֶׁר קִדְשָׁנוּ בְּמִצְוֹתָיו
וְצִוָּנוּ עַל אֲכִילַת מַצָּה:

Baruch Ata Adonai Eloheinu Melech haOlam asher kidshanu b'mitzvotav v'tzivanu al achilat matzah.

Bless you, Abba, Sovereign of all life, who provides us with this opportunity to free ourselves from sourness and selfishness with the eating of this matzah.

[*A small piece of matzah is eaten.*]

מָרוֹר
Maror
BITTER HERBS

LEADER

It is customary to mix the bitter herbs with the *charoset*, the sweet apple-and-nut mixture. In this way we acknowledge that slavery and freedom go together. We can only know the one in relation to the other. We also remind ourselves that no matter how sweet life may be, there is still the sting of suffering, and that no matter how despairing we may feel or enslaved to habits of the body, heart, and mind, there is always the promise of liberation.

COMMUNITY

בָּרוּךְ אַתָּה יְיָ אֱלֹהֵינוּ מֶלֶךְ הָעוֹלָם,
אֲשֶׁר קִדְּשָׁנוּ בְּמִצְוֹתָיו
וְצִוָּנוּ עַל אֲכִילַת מָרוֹר:

Baruch Ata Adonai Eloheinu Melech haOlam, asher kidshanu b'mitzvotav v'tzivanu al achilat maror.

Bless you Abba, Sovereign of all life, Who provides us with the opportunity to taste the bitterness of slavery that we might struggle for the sweetness of freedom. May the meal we are about to share deepen our friendship with each other and with God. And may this meal be one among many as we labor to reveal the Kingdom of God on earth through the sharing of our food.

[Make and eat a small sandwich of matzah, maror, and charoset.]

שֻׁלְחָן עוֹרֵךְ
Shulchan Aruch
DINNER IS SERVED

[As people begin to serve and eat dinner it is wise to remind them that this is a sacred meal, and that conversation should include discussions around the themes of Passover: enslavement and liberation.]

צָפוּן

Tzafon
FINDING THE HIDDEN

LEADER

Earlier in our service we hid the *afikomen*, the broken piece of matzah representing our sense of brokenness and imperfection. Now is the time for us to reclaim what is lost and move toward wholeness. We invite our younger children to hunt for and find the hidden matzah.

Jesus said, "Ask, and it will be given you; search, and you will find; knock, and the door will be opened for you" (Mt. 7:7). While our children hunt for the *afikomen*, ask God for whatever it is you need. Seek out the truth, but don't seek only—find as well. Knock on your own hardened heart that it might be opened to you and to the love of and from God that is God's freely flowing grace.

[*When the afikomen is found, a monetary reward is pledged to a charity of the child's choosing. It is appropriate to let the child announce where she or he wishes the money sent.*]

THE THIRD CUP OF WINE
[*Guests fill each other's cups with wine or grape juice.*]

LEADER

We drank the first cup in honor of fellowship, and the second in honor of freedom. We now drink our third cup in honor of courage: the courage to wage

peace as well as war, the courage to reach out with open hands rather than clenched fists, the courage to love not only our friends but our enemies as well. Jesus practiced such courage and calls us to do the same.

QUESTION

We have finished eating. Why add another glass of wine?

ANSWER

There are two reasons. First, our Passover meal satisfied our stomachs, but our souls still yearn for God. The courage to which we pledge ourselves with this third cup of wine is the courage to satisfy not only the needs of the body but also the needs of the soul.

Second, if we fully engaged each other in the spirit of Passover, recognizing our places of enslavement, we may have slipped into another kind of enslavement: prideful and judgmental thinking. We must now free ourselves from those traps and regain the greater solidarity our table fellowship is meant to create. We drink together to reaffirm the importance of people gathering together in God's Name.

COMMUNITY

בָּרוּךְ אַתָּה יְיָ, אֱלֹהֵינוּ מֶלֶךְ הָעוֹלָם,
בּוֹרֵא פְּרִי הַגָּפֶן:

Baruch Ata Adonai Eloheinu Melech haOlam borai pri hagaphen.

Bless you, Abba, Sovereign of all life, who births the fruit of the vine.

ELIJAH'S CUP

[The head table (some communities have a cup at every table) has an empty class set aside for Elijah, the prophet of peace and herald of the messiah. The glass is passed around as each guest pours some wine into Elijah's cup. The cup is then set in the center of the table.]

LEADER
This is the Cup of Elijah, the prophet of redemption.

QUESTION
Why do we fill Elijah's Cup from our own?

ANSWER
Two thousand years ago Rabbi Naftali introduced this custom saying, "Elijah is the herald of redemption, but we are the vehicles for redemption. Only when we are willing to work for the healing of the world will the prophet come and announce that the time for healing has come."

[The doors of the room are opened to the outdoors, inviting Elijah to join the seder.]

LEADER
"Lo, I will send you the prophet Elijah before the great and terrible day of the LORD comes. He will turn the hearts of parents to their children and the hearts of children to their parents" (Mal. 4:5-6).

As we invite Elijah to our fellowship meal we invite parents to hug their children and children to hug their parents, offering each other the gift of love and forgiveness. As Jesus said, "[I]f you forgive others their trespasses, your heavenly Father will also forgive you; but if you do not forgive others, neither will your Father forgive your trespasses" (Mt. 6:14).

[It is customary to sing a hymn of welcome to Elijah. Any song of healing and reconciliation would be appropriate. While the song is sung, the children are invited to come and watch the Cup of Elijah and see if the prophet does not take a sip from the cup to let all of us know that he is here and the kingdom of God is at hand. The following is the traditional Jewish welcoming of Elijah.]

ELIYAH HANAVI, (THE PROPHET ELIJAH)

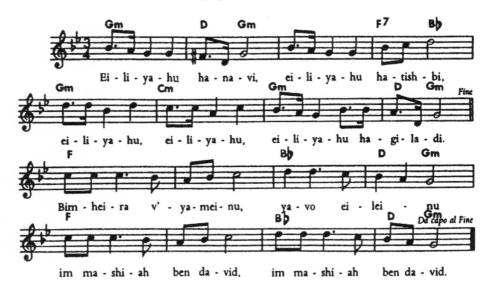

Eliyahu ha navi, Eliyahu hatishbi
Eliyahu, Eliyahu, Eliyahu hagiladi
Bim hay rah bi ya maynu, yavo aleinu
im mashiach ben David, im mashiach ben David

Elijah the Prophet, Elijah the Tishbite
Elijah, Elijah, Elijah the herald of redemption.
May the day soon come when the Messiah Son of David is among us.

בָּרֵךְ
Boraych
GRACE AFTER THE MEAL

LEADER

We praise God and give thanks for this fellowship, this meal, and this opportunity to draw closer to God.

COMMUNITY

We praise the Source of Life and devote our lives to enhancing life.

We praise the Source of Justice and devote ourselves to doing justly.

We praise the Source of Kindness and devote ourselves to acting kindly.

We praise the Source of Forgiveness and devote ourselves to forgiving others.

We praise the Source of Hope and promise never to abandon hope.

THE FOURTH CUP OF WINE

[*Guests fill each other's cups with wine or grape juice.*]

LEADER

We drink the fourth and final cup of wine in honor of peace. The Hebrew word for peace is *shalom* from the root *shalem* meaning "wholeness." Peace is not the absence of strife but the ability to engage even an enemy without losing sight of the truth that even one's enemy is part of the human family of God.

QUESTION

King David wrote, "[S]eek peace and pursue it" (Ps. 34:14 NIV). Why did he say both *seek* and *pursue*? What is the difference between these?

ANSWER

The ancient rabbis taught that we are to seek peace when peace seems near at hand, and pursue peace when peace seems far away.

QUESTION

How do we seek peace?

ANSWER

We seek peace when we invite those with whom we struggle to sit at our table and share food and fellowship.

QUESTION

How do we pursue peace?

ANSWER

We pursue peace when we leave the safety of our table and meet the other halfway. We pursue peace when, like Jesus, we go even further and seek out the estranged where they live.

COMMUNITY

בָּרוּךְ אַתָּה יְיָ, אֱלֹהֵינוּ מֶלֶךְ הָעוֹלָם,
בּוֹרֵא פְּרִי הַגָּפֶן:

Baruch Ata Adonai Eloheinu Melech haOlam borai pri hagaphen.

Bless you, Abba, Sovereign of all life, who births the fruit of the vine.

נִרְצָה
Nirtzah
CONCLUSION

LEADER

For thousands of years the Jewish people have remembered and listened to the call of liberation. Tonight we, too, are honored to hear that call.

COMMUNITY

Tonight we remember the bitterness of slavery. Not only the enslavement of the Hebrews to Pharaoh, but our own enslavement to power, greed, and pride; to labels, logos, and manufactured needs; and to sour habits of thought, word, and deed that rob us of dignity and incite us to rob others of the same.

LEADER

Let us stand, join hands and hearts, and honor the call of Passover: the call to accept God's gift of freedom. Let us rise up with courage and grasp hold of freedom that we might fashion a world more strongly committed to justice, kindness, and humility—which was and is the way of the prophets and of Jesus.

COMMUNITY

"Lord, make me an instrument of your peace. Where there is hatred, let me sow peace; where there is injury, let me sow forgiveness; where there is doubt, let me sow faith; where there is despair, let me give hope; where there is darkness, let me give light; where there is sadness, let me give joy"
(Prayer attributed to St. Francis).

LEADER
Go in peace.

Let Us Break Bread Together

FURTHER READING

We recommend the following books to those who would like to learn more about the Jewish Passover seder, its traditions, history, and contemporary use in Judaism.

Women's Passover Companion
Edited by Rabbi Sharon Cohen Anisfeld, Tara Mohr, and Catherine Spector
Jewish Lights Publishing, 2004

Creating Lively Passover Seders: An Interactive Sourcebook of Tales, Texts, and Activities
David Arnow
Jewish Lights Publishing, 2004

The Passover Table: New and Traditional Recipes for Your Seders and the Entire Passover Week
Susan Friedland
Quill, 1994

Make Your Own Passover Seder: A New Approach to Creating a Personal Family Celebration
Alan Abraham Kay, Jo Kay
Jossey-Bass, 2004

Studies on the Haggadah: From the Teachings of Nechama Leibowitz
Nechama Leibowitz,
Urim Publications, 2002

Keeping Passover: Everything You Need to Know to Bring the Ancient Tradition to Life
Ira Steingroot
HarperSanFrancisco, 1995

Passover: The Family Guide to Spiritual Celebration
Dr. Ron Wolfson
Jewish Lights Publishing, 2002

About Paraclete Press

Who We Are

Paraclete Press is an ecumenical publisher of books on Christian spirituality for people of all denominations and backgrounds.

We publish books that represent the wide spectrum of Christian belief and practice—from Catholic to Evangelical to liturgical to Orthodox.

We market our books primarily through booksellers; we are what is called a "trade" publisher, which means that we like it best when readers buy our books from booksellers, our partners in successfully reaching as wide of an audience as possible.

We are uniquely positioned in the marketplace without connection to large corporation or a conglomerate and with informal relationships to many branches and denominations of faith, rather than a formal relationship to any single one. We focus on publishing a diversity of thoughts and perspectives—the fruit of our diversity as a company.

What We Are Doing

Paraclete Press is publishing books that show the diversity and depth of what it means to be Christian. We publish books that reflect the Christian experience across many cultures, time periods, and houses of worship.

We publish books about spiritual practice, history, ideas, customs and rituals, and books that nourish the vibrant life of the church.

We have several different series of books within Paraclete Press, including the bestselling Living Library series of modernized classic texts, A Voice from the Monastery—giving voice to men and women monastics on what it means to live a spiritual life today, and Many Mansions—for exploring the riches of the world's religious traditions and discovering how other faiths inform Christian thought and practice.

Learn more about us at our website: www.paracletepress.com or call us toll-free at (800) 451-5006.

If you liked *Let Us Break Bread Together*, you will also enjoy:

MUDHOUSE SABBATH

Lauren F. Winner, author of *Girl Meets God*
144 pages
ISBN: 1-55725-344-7
$17.95, Hardcover

Despite her conversion from Orthodox Judaism to Christianity, Lauren Winner finds that her life is still shaped by the spiritual essences of Judaism—rich traditions and religious practices that she can't leave behind. In *Mudhouse Sabbath*, this compelling young writer illuminates eleven spiritual practices that can transform the way we view the world, and God. Whether discussing her own prayer life, the spirituality of candle-lighting, or the differences between the Jewish Sabbath and a Sunday spent at the Mudhouse, her favorite coffee shop, Winner writes with appealing honesty and rare insight.

"At a time when we are so aware of the differences between Judaism and Christianity, Lauren Winner's book on what we can learn from each other is refreshingly welcome."
    —Rabbi Harold Kushner, author of *When Bad Things Happen to Good People*

"A writer of spiritual substance and grace-filled style."
    —*Publishers Weekly*

"A little book that glows with warmth and tender charm as it appreciates the wisdom of a 'different' culture."
    —*Booklist*

HOW FIRM A FOUNDATION:
A GIFT OF JEWISH WISDOM FOR CHRISTIANS AND JEWS

Rabbi Yechiel Eckstein
269 pages
ISBN: 1-55725-189-3
$16.95, Trade Paper

How is the Jewish Sabbath observed? What are Passover and Yom Kippur all about: My children have been invited to a friend's bar mitzvah. Should they bring a gift? What should they do, or not do?

Rabbi Eckstein, popular teacher to both Jewish and Christian audiences, answers these questions and much more. Through his rich presentation of Jewish life—beliefs and practices, festivals and holy days, important Jewish life cycle events and occasions—you will come to understand what is distinctive about Judaism and Jewish life, as well as what Jews and Christians share in common.

"Rich in information Christians need to know to be responsible and affirming friends, neighbors and fellow citizens to Jewish people . . . Most important of all, this book is brimming with Jewish wisdom that will enrich and strengthen your faith."
    —From the foreword by Dr. Lloyd John Ogilvie, former Chaplain, United States Senate.

Available from most booksellers or through Paraclete Press:
www.paracletepress.com, 1-800-451-5006.
Try your local bookstore first.